THE GEOGRAPHY OF AIR TRANSPORT

UNIVERSITY LIBRARY OF GEOGRAPHY

edited by

W. G. EAST

Professor of Geography

in the University of London

THE
GEOGRAPHY
OF
AIR TRANSPORT

Kenneth R. Sealy

READER IN GEOGRAPHY

AT THE LONDON SCHOOL OF ECONOMICS AND POLITICAL SCIENCE

ALDINE PUBLISHING COMPANY / *Chicago*

387.7
S 438

First U.S. edition published 1968 by
ALDINE Publishing Company
320 West Adams Street
Chicago, Illinois 60606

Hutchison & Co. Ltd., London

Library of Congress Catalog Card Number 68-19872

Printed in the United States of America

CONTENTS

MAPS AND DIAGRAMS

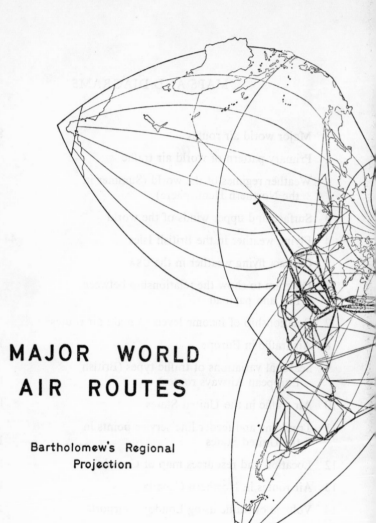

MAJOR WORLD
AIR ROUTES

Bartholomew's Regional
Projection

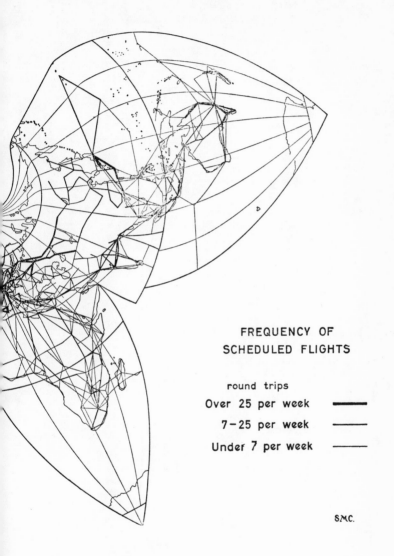

FREQUENCY OF
SCHEDULED FLIGHTS

round trips

Over 25 per week ━━━━

7 – 25 per week ────

Under 7 per week ───

S.M.C.

TABLES

PREFACE TO SECOND EDITION

I would like to express my thanks to Mr R. S. Doganis for his invaluable help in revising the statistics, and for the preparation of the new map of European air routes; and to Mrs E. Wilson and Miss E. A. Crux for drawing the maps.

London, January 1965   K.R.S.

PREFACE TO FIRST EDITION

My thanks are due to many people who have so freely given their assistance in the preparation of this book. I am particularly indebted to the following: the editors of the series, Professor R. O. Buchanan, the late Dr A. H. Fox, and to Mr G. J. Ponsonby for reading through the text and for many helpful suggestions; Mr D. C. Young for his invaluable aid in the collection of material; Mrs E. Wilson and Miss S. M. Chantler for drawing the maps and diagrams.

Acknowledgement is also made for permission to reproduce the following material: Mr John Bartholomew for the use of the regional projection in the map of major world air routes; Dr J. Parker Van Zandt and the Brookings Institution, Washington, DC, for *Fig. 1*; Mr Glenn Cunningham and the Association of American Geographers for *Fig. 5*; Dr W. S. Barry and the University of London for *Fig. 10*; the editor of *Geography* for allowing me to reproduce *Figs. 14* and *15* which first appeared in a paper by the author in *Geography* (1955). Acknowledgement is made in the text for the use of statistical data. Statistical data from official sources and the Crown copyright meterological data used in the construction of *Figs. 3* and *4* are reproduced by kind permission of the Controller of H.M. Stationery Office.

Perhaps I ought to explain that the small superior figures that appear in the text are intended to refer readers to the list of publications to be found at the end of each chapter, where details concerning the particular book or paper are given.

London, October 1956   K.R.S.

Part One

I

INTRODUCTION

In spite of a hurried existence in a turbulent world, all of us still try to find some time to sit and dream. Men have always built their castles in the air and dreamed of the 'impossible'—whether it be the reason for their existence, or, more prosaically, the quest for riches, or the desire to fly like the birds. Travel and exploration have long been fruitful subjects upon which to dream, and much that we now take for granted must once have been a dream. Fortunately, perhaps, men have constantly wanted to know what lay beyond the horizon.

To the people of the civilized world of Greece and Rome, Britain was the northern end of a misty frontier that extended south to the Pillars of Hercules and the sands of the Sahara. In the centuries that followed, that concept remained largely un-altered until the outburst of activity we call the 'Age of Dis-covery'. The achievements of the fifteenth and sixteenth centuries are too well known to need elaboration here, but it is curious to remember that two of the dreams of that age were destined to remain fruitless until the present century—the conquest of the North-West and North-East Passages. With the activity of the colonizing powers of Europe in the eighteenth and nineteenth centuries, the thread is continued right up to modern times when the final phase in the exploration of the planet seems imminent.

Of the many lessons that may be learnt from such a record, two points seem especially important at the moment. In the first place, it is no accident that the periods of intense exploratory or colonizing activity were also periods of advance in other spheres. The importance of 'place' and more particularly, the ease with which one can travel from one place to another, is an essential ingredient in an expanding economy. 'Accessibility' is part and parcel of man's material progress.

Secondly, movement implies a means of locomotion, and each of the great historical periods of discovery or colonization is linked with a major step in transport development. The Elizabethan navigator could never have circumnavigated the globe in a vessel rigged like a Roman galley. True oceanic voyages required a vessel able to take advantage of any wind and capable of sailing over a wide range of direction with any given wind. Further, the vessel had to be big enough to carry the necessary stores while remaining manœuvrable enough to permit accurate navigation. Such a ship was the caravel of Columbus.

In turn, the steamship, the railway and the automobile have made their contributions. All are essentially extensions of the older modes of transport. Man with these vehicles could move himself, as well as bulky articles, with expedition, and, just as important, with regularity. Great as these modern achievements are, they demand no new attitude of mind. Land and sea are two elements. To get from one to the other involves transhipment, so that the geographical disposition of land masses and water bodies is a major consideration. Some nations have developed a 'maritime' outlook—closely linked by a long coastline, or an island site—to sea travel and trade. Others, far from such sites, have become 'continental', their life oriented to an existence that makes fewer demands on sea-borne trade.

Against this background must one judge the impact of the aeroplane. In a very real sense, the aeroplane knows no barrier. It moves in the continuum of the atmosphere which is both three-dimensional and relatively uniform. Its appeal is to 'maritime' and 'continental' nations alike, and here, surely, lies the key to the aeroplane's place in the world. By the use of the terms 'maritime' and 'continental', I have tried to suggest a limitation in the accessibility of one place with another imposed by the older forms of transport. The aeroplane bridges the gap and is, therefore, but a further extension of the older forms of transport—perhaps the final extension. We should remember, too, that we are so close to the birth of aviation that we cannot as yet see how it will affect the fortunes of nations which were built and continue to exist through the medium of surface movement. We have the means to fill the gap, but as yet the bridge is tenuous.

From such preliminary considerations, we may now expand the discussion a stage further. Transport is necessary to satisfy the function of 'place', or as Bonavia[2] has defined it—'transport aims at creating utility of place'. Without a means of transport territorial specialization is impossible, and, therefore, civilization as we know it. Without it, communities must exist solely on local resources and the density of population is dependent upon those resources. Just how close is the relation between transport and economic development may be seen by glancing at the history of civilizations past and present. Thus water transport is the simplest form of bulk transport and all the early civilizations, e.g. those of the Mediterranean Lands, depended on it. The fact that all 'water sites' were not important, demonstrates the influence of other factors besides transport. The conquest of the land masses really began with the railway and is essentially a nineteenth-century phenomenon. With the bulk-carrying capacity of the railway available, the interiors of the continents became accessible and the rise of the big continental nations of the twentieth century begins in this era. With the added resources made available by the railway, trade becomes more truly 'World' trade and with it an increase in population density is feasible and industrialism a possibility. The automobile and aeroplane represent the final stage in mobility, the former finding its place particularly as a flexible short-haul medium and the latter for speedy long-distance movement.

The importance of place in the economic sense springs from three familiar facts, namely:

(a) The unequal distribution of resources.
(b) The unequal distribution of population.
(c) The unequal development of knowledge among men of how to utilize material resources.

The proportion of factors required to produce a given commodity varies, just as the demand for that commodity varies, from place to place. Ideally, each area should produce 'what best it can' in the light of the facts given in (a), (b) and (c) above. This is simply the Law of Comparative Costs. It follows, too, that trade will not develop between areas unless the differences in the prices of goods in each of those areas is sufficient to cover the cost of transport between them. Regional differences in wage levels, and in such things as the level of skill, must also play a part. Trade then demands :

(a) Availability of goods themselves.
(b) Wide knowledge of the prices of those goods.
(c) Means of transport.

Having shown how transport enters the field of human activity, we must now admit that any attempt to determine how transport costs will influence trade is fraught with difficulty. The assumption that such costs are proportionately related to distance is far too simple, as is the assumption that transport costs increase at a decreasing rate with distance. In any case, any application of the Law of Comparative Costs in terms of cost alone ignores many important, if less tangible, elements, e.g. perishability. Where market conditions are competitive, transport charges may be taken as reflecting costs. Under monopoly conditions the relationship is obscured, since charges will include a proportion of monopoly profit. Government policies affect the issue, particularly where the attempt is made to influence the balance of investment and consumption. Thus in under-developed countries investment will be greater in relation to consumption than in developed territories. Transport (and the export industries) may be subsidized in under-developed countries—an 'infant transport' protection. One should note, finally, that it is unwise to speak generally in terms of goods and services. Questions of bulk, perishability, or value per unit weight, are important, while the fact that some goods lose weight during manufacture is also relevant.

In the chapters that follow we shall consider in some detail the technical and economic characteristics of air transport in order to appreciate how traffic is generated and where. Before we can discuss the pattern of routes in any area of the world, we must try to discover why air transport is essentially a high-cost medium. In the light of this, we must consider the type of cargo for which it is best suited under all sorts of conditions that apply in the world. Finally, we must consider briefly the use of maps and projections in the study of air transport.

Maps in an air age

The flexibility of the aeroplane, and its ability to fly directly between any two points on the globe that lie within its range of operation, makes great demands on the ability to use maps effectively. Whereas the ubiquity of maps drawn on the Mercator projection has receded since World War II, too many of us still think of the world in terms of the distortions inherent in any flat representation of its surface. Raise your eyes for a moment and call up your own mental picture of the world. What do you see? By the shortest route, does North America lie west of Asia? Is the North Pole the centre of the land hemisphere? Is New York or London nearer to Tokyo? Does Hanoi lie west of New York? It must be confessed that many of us would plump for the wrong answer in some cases.

Air transport is much concerned with the relationship of the land masses and with the shortest and most direct routes between them. This is not always realized, since surface transport up to now has had perforce to employ a strong east–west component in its movement, because of the inhospitable nature of the polar regions and the northern parts of the great land masses of North America and Euro-Asia. The aeroplane is now quite capable of overcoming these difficulties should trade warrant it. The short-comings of some maps tends also to distort the globe in an east–west direction—the prime example being the map of the world on Mercator's projection. Enough has been said to suggest the limitations and we may now turn to consider how the map may be used in a study of air transport.

One of our primary requirements is a map of world air routes and since aircraft can fly directly, such routes should approximate to great circle tracks. In addition, the distance between destina-tions should be accurately portrayed. This apparently simple requirement is in fact the hardest of all to realize. Reasonable accuracy can be achieved for a hemisphere, but beyond a hemi-sphere the globe curves in again towards the other pole, while a flat map must continue to expand outwards. As Van Zandt has pointed out,[7] most of the world's activity does in fact take place within a hemisphere. We shall return to this concept at a later stage, but here we may note that a hemisphere may be reasonably portrayed on a map.

For the representation of a hemisphere the azimuthal group of projections is the most useful (*Fig. 1*). If possible we should like to be able to show great circle routes as straight lines on the map and be able to measure distance along them. The Gnomonic projection is the only one that shows great circles as straight lines, but it severely distorts practically everything else. Hence the calculation of distance is a complicated task. Even for a hemisphere only, no projection can show both distance and direction correctly over the whole area depicted. The Zenithal Equidistant projection —a cousin of the Gnomonic—can show both for one point at least —the centre of the projection. This implies that straight lines radiating from the centre represent great circles in their true direction or azimuth, and distances along these lines is uniform

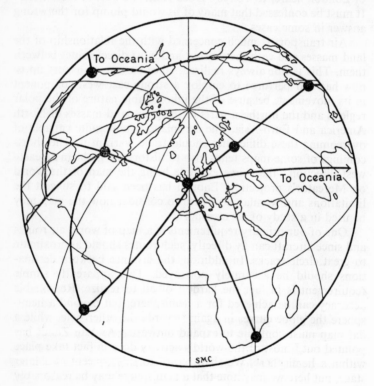

PRIMARY PATTERN OF WORLD AIR TRAFFIC

Zenithal Equidistant Proj.   *After Van Zandt.*

Figure 1

if not correct in scale. With the aid of a special nomograph—like the one developed by Van Zandt or Harrison[5]—we can determine the path of great circles other than those that pass through the centre. Such tracks will be curves, of course. The merit of this projection lies not only in its portrayal of great circle tracks, but also in the fact that its distortion of other properties, e.g. shape and area, is small compared with that of any other type of projection. A nomograph also enables distance to be measured on this projection.

So far we have been considering only a hemisphere. When we attempt to show the whole world on one map, our difficulties increase enormously. We can, of course, portray it as two hemispheres drawn on the Zenithal Equidistant projection with centres at the two poles respectively. This destroys the relationship between the hemispheres and makes the portrayal of routes that overlap both hemispheres unconvincing.

The azimuthal projections we have been discussing may be modified to produce a world picture. To construct a Gnomonic or Zenithal Equidistant projection we imagine that a plate is placed at right angles to the Earth's surface and touching it at one point, i.e. it is tangential. The projection of the Earth's features on to the flat plate represents the basis of our map. We may alter this representation mathematically to offset distortion —as the Zenithal Equidistant does in the case of scale. Nevertheless, it will be realized that the hemisphere is the limit of such projections—since the tangent of the globe at 90 degrees from the point of contact is infinity. However, there is no reason why more than one plate should not be placed tangentially on to the Earth's surface. Thus the world may be considered as projected on to the walls of a 'box' enclosing it and forming, therefore, six gnomonic projections. Once the impression has been made, the box may be flattened out to produce a somewhat odd-looking map. This Cubic projection is used in a modified form in the Olympic map of Taylor and Campbell.[6] In place of the cube or box, more complicated figures may be used with more than six sides and projections using Tetrahedrons and Icosahedrons have been constructed.[3],[4] The Icosahedral projection, for example, 'opens out' into twenty triangular surfaces, and on each of these, great circles will be straight lines, since each triangle is a small gnomonic and has that projection's properties.

All these projections fail to produce a uniformly compact

map, for they appear as a series of partially joined pieces or gores. More important, each gore is a law unto itself and where routes cross from one gore to another, the direction changes. Thus it is at the intersection of the gores that the trouble arises. Moreover, whereas the great circle bearing is moderately well shown, distance is usually very much more difficult to ascertain than on the simpler hemisphere of the Zenithal Equidistant.

The other families of projections may also be modified for our purposes. The cylindrical group, of which the Mercator is one example, is a case in point. Botley[3] has produced an Oblique Gore Cylindrical that shows great circle routes moderately well on what looks like four slices of orange peel. In addition, this map shows areas in their correct proportion. Finally, Bartholomew[1] has produced several projections suitable for World maps, including the Regional and Nordic projections. The former is the projection used for the map of World air routes on pages 8–9 of this book.

It will be seen that all these projections have severe limitations, and many world maps are arranged as gores. For general purposes this does not matter—since one can appreciate the relationship of the major features of the Earth's surface from them. For more precise determination of direction and distance, the Zenithal Equidistant projection of the world as two hemispheres, used with a corrected scale made from the nomographs of Van Zandt and others, is sound.

Before we leave this problem, it might be as well to consider the Mercator projection and its properties. Why did it become so popular? To understand this we must consider the problems of navigation. Whereas the great circle is the shortest possible route between any two points on the globe, it is not possible for either a ship or an aircraft to follow such a route directly. In order to pursue a given course a vessel must have some point of reference with which it can check its progress in a directional sense. The magnetic poles have long performed this task through the use of a compass. In order to steer a course between two points, it is necessary to be able to keep that course as constant as possible. A great circle track is a track of constantly changing bearing and would entail numerous small changes of course with relation to the compass in order to follow it. Hence most vessels and aircraft approximate the great circle track as far as possible by steering a series of courses. Each course will have a constant bearing.

Lines of constant bearing on the globe are called rhumb lines, so that navigation by ordinary compass requires a chart that shows lines of constant bearing as straight lines. Unfortunately, it is impossible in the nature of things to show both great circles and rhumb lines as straight lines on the same chart. Of the two, the navigator requires the latter for plotting his courses and his work is simplified if he can draw them as straight lines. He must put up with the fact that the great circle will appear as a curve.

The Mercator projection is the answer, since straight lines drawn upon it are lines of constant bearing, i.e. rhumb lines. In addition, distance in an east–west direction can be directly measured and only a simple correction is needed for measuring distance in a north–south sense. Shape is shown as accurately as is possible on any projection, but the areas of the lands and seas are grossly inaccurate. This is the price paid for its other properties. As a navigational projection, then, it is ideal, and this was the purpose for which it was originally constructed. Comparison between a great circle track and its rhumb line approximation is difficult in any case, but on the Mercator projection the problem can be overcome by the use of mathematical corrections. As a track on the Mercator, the great circle will appear as a curve.

So far we have considered the use of maps for showing world air routes and have touched upon their navigational uses. Radio aids are an important aspect of modern air navigation, and pose their own requirements. We might perhaps summarize the methods of navigation generally in order to appreciate the problem in its entirety.

Methods of air navigation

(a) Visual contact. Map-reading.

(b) Dead-reckoning navigation (DR). Use of True Airspeed of the aircraft and a knowledge of the prevailing wind velocity to plot the aircraft's track over the ground and its rate of travel with respect to the ground (ground speed—G/s). Use is made of visual and radio checks etc. to fix position at intervals.

(c) Astro-navigation. Estimation of position with reference to the heavenly bodies. Essentially an additional aid to DR navigation.

(d) Radio Direction Finding. Use of radio signals from known ground stations to fix position.

(e) Radio Range. Use of radio beams as 'airways' and landing aids.

(*f*) Omni-range. Use of radio beams sent out in all directions by ground stations for position fixing.

(*g*) Radar or Hyperbolic Systems. Use of radio impulses to determine bearing and position. In modern systems, distance from the station may also be found, as in the Distance Measuring Equipment (DME) and R THETA systems.

In our discussion of the Mercator projection we were in fact considering the requirements of (*b*) and (*c*) above. The calculation of course and track is made with reference to the compass, and rhumb lines should appear as straight lines to aid the calculation. When we enter the sphere of radio navigation the requirement alters somewhat, for radio impulses travel from station to aircraft along the shortest route—i.e. the great circle.

In radio navigation the Zenithal Equidistant projection again comes into its own. The centre of the projection is placed over the position of the radio station, whence the direction of all radio impulses from that station may be directly plotted. For measuring distance, use is made of the time taken for the impulse to travel from station to aircraft and since the impulse travels a great circle course, the distance will be the great circle distance. The basis for most radio charts is, therefore, either a Zenithal Equidistant projection or a modification of it for specific purposes.

When one comes to deal with particular continents or countries of the world—either to show air routes or for navigation—the problem becomes much easier, since it is far simpler to represent a small section of a globe on a flat surface than the whole. Many projections have been evolved for depicting various aspects of regional development. For our purposes it need only be remembered that a projection must be chosen that shows direction and distance as accurately as possible. In very small areas, such as the British Isles, the choice of projection is least important. The conical group are satisfactory and the Transverse Mercator of the Ordnance Survey is adequate for most purposes. Before taking leave of our maps, it is a useful exercise to take the map drawn inside the covers and consider the wider implications of geographical position. The aeroplane has made all points on the Earth nearer to each other, as can be appreciated by plotting the distance one may travel in an hour by train, ship and aeroplane. Remember, too, that the last named can fly directly and is not hampered by coastal transhipment. Certain areas will find themselves more strategically placed than others. Thus Britain and Europe find themselves in the centre of the land hemisphere and are likely to retain and, indeed, increase their stature as route foci. It is hardly surprising that London Airport handles such an enormous variety of traffic, some of it 'staging' through London on its way to other points on the globe. As a contrast, we may consider another island—Newfoundland—until the coming of the aeroplane of little consequence in the transport world. Gander Airport, Newfoundland, used to record a large number of aircraft movements as the result of its position off the eastern seaboard of Canada. With the advent of aircraft capable of flying the Atlantic non-stop, its importance has waned in recent years.

Similarly, one may find other 'outposts' that break up long ocean hauls, e.g. Hawaii, the Azores and the island chains of the East and West Indies. Not only islands, but peninsular sites like Lisbon and Singapore, and mid-continental sites like Edmonton and Winnipeg, have taken on a world significance. With the technical advance of the aeroplane, some of these places may enjoy only a passing importance, but many are likely to remain as key sites in the world pattern.

There is an interesting comparison to be drawn here between these 'air-staging points' and the older steamship 'coaling stations'. The points concerned are rarely coincident, for the requirements of the two forms of transport are different, but the history of such coaling stations as Aden and Cape Town may be pointers to the future of their aircraft equivalents. Those that survive will almost surely lie near the great circle trunk routes of the world.

REFERENCES

1. Bartholomew, J. *The Comparative Atlas*. (Meiklejohn, 1950.)
2. Bonavia, M. R. *The Economics of Transport*. (London, 1936.)
3. Botley, F. V. 'The Tetrahedral Gnomonic Projection', *Geography*, Vol. 34, 1949.
   Botley, F. V. 'A new Map of World Air Routes', *New Commonwealth*, 1951.
4. Fisher, Irving. 'The Icosahedral Projection', *Geographical Review*, Vol. 33, 1943.
5. Harrison, R. E. 'The Nomograph as an Instrument in Map Making', *Geographical Review*, Vol. 33, 1943.
6. Taylor, E. G. R., and Campbell, E. M. J. *Olympic Air Age World Map*. (Philip, 1946.)
7. Van Zandt, J. Parker. *The Geography of World Air Transport*. (Brookings Institution, Washington, D.C., 1944.)

2

THE PHYSICAL GEOGRAPHY OF AVIATION

In the early days of aviation before World War I, a strong breeze was calculated to make most aircraft of the period somewhat uncomfortable to handle, and it was true to say that the moods of the atmosphere dictated the situation. We have come a long way since that time, and today it is all too easy to dismiss the impact of physical conditions as a mere trifle. It cannot be too strongly emphasized that this is just not true. As aircraft fly higher and faster, new problems replace old ones and the battle continues. Since the medium in which the aeroplane operates is the atmosphere, it is only natural that the majority of problems are concerned with weather and climate. Nevertheless, aircraft must still start and finish their journeys upon the Earth's surface, and topographical considerations are not unimportant.

The three most vital assets of the aeroplane stem from its use of the atmosphere in which to travel. In the first place land and sea junctions cease to be major physical elements in the traffic pattern, as we have already suggested in Chapter 1. Transhipment of cargo at coastal ports is avoided by the use of aircraft—a saving in time and money, which can be critical for certain classes of goods. Less tangible is the fact that the coastlines of the world have lost something of their importance as dividing lines between states, encouraging greater inter-state co-operation not only in military and political fields, but in commerce too. The effective market area may be increased, or, failing that, at least a greater contact is possible between traders. Apart from an immunity from coastal transhipment, aircraft are freer also from the grosser topographical elements that hinder land transport.

The second asset is just as important, i.e. the speed of travel. 'Speed' in this context implies not only a saving in time, but also in distance, since the aircraft normally travels more directly. Of all the possible media for transport, the atmosphere offers the least resistance to the passage of a moving body and the aeroplane benefits accordingly. The effect of this increase in speed is to bring all points on the Earth's surface closer together in time.

Finally, travel in the air needs no road or track. This is of supreme importance in difficult terrain, where the laying of roads and railways has been an almost prohibitive proposition. The exploitation of under-developed territories will undoubtedly be vastly quickened by the use of aircraft, and new resources badly needed by the world at large may now be more easily assessed.

All these benefits are not conferred without penalty. In order to travel freely in the air, an aeroplane must first raise itself off the ground, and thereafter sustain its position according to the plan of the flight. In order to take-off it must overcome the pull of gravity. Herein lies its chief weakness, for in order to accomplish free flight it must do a great deal of work. Thus a compact, light but powerful engine is required, a need met by the aero-engine at the expense of fuel consumption. In order to accommodate the necessary fuel a much smaller space and weight is available for the carriage of cargo—'payload'. It is a characteristic feature of the machine that its payload represents a very small proportion of its total weight in comparison with surface vehicles. It follows then that the longer the flight, the greater the fuel load and the smaller the payload. This represents Nature's toll for the freedom of movement available.

The Earth's surface features affect the aeroplane in two main contexts, (a) in the vicinity of airfields, and (b) during the actual transit. The first is important enough to merit separate discussion and is dealt with in Chapter 8. We might just note that since the majority of airfields serve densely populated areas, and these areas are predominantly lowlands, the problems are concerned chiefly with local topography rather than the major relief obstacles. In the actual transit, relief influences the situation far less. Very high mountains—especially the Himalayas—still form a potent deterrent. This is not so much because of their height alone, as the effect they produce on weather conditions. This is an important consideration, for any disturbance that arises is felt at altitudes much greater than those of the peaks themselves. In addition, turbulence, cloud and precipitation render an emergency descent almost impossible even supposing the terrain itself permitted this. It goes without saying that the lack of settlement does not improve matters either. The prime example is provided by the Himalayas, Pamir and Nan Shan ranges of southern Asia, which, strung east–west across the continent, divide air routes into two separate spheres and thus reduce north–south accessibility. One further point may be demonstrated by taking the Western Cordilleras of the American continents as examples. With some exceptions, most of these ranges do not approach the altitudes of the Himalayas yet they are important elements. In the Americas, the ranges trend north–south across the dominant line of movement of intruding air masses, so that their influence on weather conditions is far greater than their altitude alone might suggest.

High mountains are hazards, therefore, not primarily as the result of altitude alone, but also because of their difficult relief and lack of settlement, and because of their influence on weather. Altitude alone can affect the siting of airports, and is an important consideration in the case of plateau sites, e.g. in East Africa. At altitudes above approximately 200 ft. above mean sea level, the fall-off in aircraft performance at take-off can mean a reduction in the possible load that can be carried.

Mountainous areas also tend to distort radio and radar beams, either by obstruction, or by 'bending', the latter the result of the metalliferous content of the structures 'attracting' the beam and so rendering it inaccurate. Radio aids are doubly necessary in these areas for reasons we have just considered. Airports sited near mountains suffer most and the author was aware of at least one 'bent' radio beam in the vicinity of Vancouver during the last war.

A discussion of the dangers of mountainous areas brings us naturally to the wider problem of forced descent and alternative landing grounds. We should note at once that this is a matter of declining importance as technique improves. Deserts have pecularities of their own apart from their isolation from human communities. Once again the meteorological influence can be important. Apart from dust storms arising from convectional instability, most deserts suffer from poor visibility in the form of haze that may extend to the 10,000-ft. level. The means of survival are poor, and it is not surprising that air routes over the bigger deserts are few and far between, with the possible exception of the Western Sahara. The old flying-boat route from Cairo to South Africa followed the line of the Nile and the lakes of Central and Eastern Africa for very good reasons. It is worth emphasizing that flying boats rather than landplanes were used since water landing sites were freely available, and, just as important, entailed no vast constructional effort in a continent ill-equipped for such measures. Since 1945 the greater range of modern machines and their increased reliability have warranted the use of landplanes.

Forested zones, especially those within the Tropics or the northern Taiga, present little real obstruction. Forced descent may be a hazardous business, but the presence of lakes and rivers mitigates these perils. This is particularly true of the glaciated territory in Canada and the USSR. Indeed the presence of numerous lakes in these areas has helped rather than hindered air traffic. The much wider use of seaplanes that can be converted to make use of skis enables lakes to be used more effectively. In the forested areas of the Tropics the position is less favourable. The effect of a dense plant cover on weather phenomena has still to be completely studied, but the influence is there. Nevertheless, most air routes skirt the forests of the Amazon basin for similar reasons that deserts are avoided—there is no traffic, and survival on descent is difficult if not impossible.

In conclusion we must remember that the aeroplane has one excellent trump card—it needs no track to be laid and maintained across difficult terrain. On the other hand, it requires an airport and is guided in flight by ground-located radio aids, both affected by topography. Its freedom, therefore, is relative rather than absolute.

In order to demonstrate the influence of relief in an actual case, we may consider the route from Buenos Aires to Santiago across the Andes. Three possible routes exist in this instance: one is direct, and the others lie north and south of the direct passage. By following the direct great circle track, a distance of 606 nautical miles must be covered, but the aircraft has to cross the Andes at between 22,500 and 24,500 ft. above sea level. Since Santiago at 1,700 ft. is situated so close to the mountains, the aircraft arrives over the city with up to 20,000 ft. to spare and must waste an hour letting down slowly to the airport. Any attempt at a rapid descent causes discomfort to the passengers.

The southerly route is more circuitous and is 716 nautical miles in length. It crosses the Andes at a lower level than the direct route, some 120 miles south of Santiago. With fine weather the crossing may be made at only 14,000 ft. above sea level. On the other hand, with high winds, which may reach 100 knots at 26,000 ft., a minimum altitude of 18,000 ft. must be held in order to avoid severe downdraughts on the eastern side and updraughts on the western side of the mountains. The latter help the climb out of Santiago on the eastbound run. The northern route, finally, is still longer at 799 nautical miles, but enjoys better weather conditions than the other two. The height of the Andes here means that the aircraft must cross at between 21,000 and 24,000 ft.

In fine weather, the southern route has much to recommend it and is normally used, but where weather conditions are poor, the northerly passage is usually a safer and more reliable transit. The close link between mountains and weather conditions is an important one and we shall return to consider its full implications in the sphere of meteorology at a later stage.

Weather is of far greater importance to the aviator than difficulties of terrain. To the earthbound human being, only the lowest few thousand feet of the atmosphere appear to matter and we are all familiar with charts that depict the various elements of weather and climate at the Earth's surface. The modern airliner, on the other hand, may operate between the ground and anything up to 30,000 ft. above sea level. Surface conditions are still important, for the machine must eventually return to its airport, but for expeditious operations, the upper atmosphere is just as important. Until the advent of the aeroplane, little was known about the atmosphere above about 10,000 ft. and it must be admitted that our knowledge of the upper air is still sketchy. It is ironical, perhaps, but modern research into upper air conditions is helping us to understand the mechanism of surface weather, for many of the disturbances affecting the surface have their origin in the upper layers.

Before considering regional characteristics, we must first be aware of the elements of weather that particularly influence aviation. Strictly speaking, all elements are important in the sense that each contributes to the whole that we call 'weather', but some elements are more critical than others. Weather is not only a hazard, but has its beneficial side also, e.g. winds may expedite a journey as well as delay one. Further, as technique advances, the dangers arising from weather conditions tend to recede.

The elements of weather may be summarized as temperature, pressure and water content. From the first two, air density may be calculated (Boyle's Law) and wind systems charted. Water content controls cloud formation and precipitation. Pressure differences, arising from unequal temperature distribution, give rise to wind—a very important element to an airman. Wind will affect an aircraft's speed with relation to the ground and hence its range and payload. Airport layout must take into account prevailing winds, since modern aircraft generally take-off and land against the wind, even though considerable cross-wind components can be dealt with. Wind has two components—direction and speed—forming wind velocity (w/v). Wind velocity results not only from pressure differences, but is also affected by the Earth's rotation.

Temperature distribution in the atmosphere, apart from instigating the world's weather, is the chief element controlling the formation of fog and icing conditions. In addition, aero-engines are sensitive to temperature change and their efficiency is affected.

Air density is a determinant of the lifting capacity of a wing. Broadly, the lower the density, the lower the lift generated by a wing at any given airspeed. Thus to maintain lift, the machine must fly faster. By the same token, where density is low, the take-off and landing speeds will be higher. Density will fluctuate according to either temperature or pressure changes, while humidity will also affect it. In hot desert areas, therefore, density will be lower than in temperate zones. Indeed, the Tropics as a whole are the regions where this consideration is an important one. Aircraft built in England are sent to the Sudan or Libya for tropical trials under high-temperature and low-density conditions. Since pressure falls with height, density will also decrease with altitude (roughly air density decreases by 10% for every 3,000 feet gained. At 20,000 ft., therefore, density is about half its surface value). This not only affects high-altitude operations— perhaps over mountain ranges—but also the siting of airports in high plateaux.

So long as the moisture content in the air remains as water vapour, it is invisible and normally of little consequence to aviation. Problems arise when condensation and precipitation occur, bringing cloud and poor visibility, and if temperatures are suitable, icing conditions and fog. The chief situations that give rise to widespread phenomena of this kind are to be found in frontal zones (*Fig. 2*), or where convectional instability and orographic influence are characteristic. Visibility deteriorates in cloud, which may be found at all levels up to the Tropopause, and may be associated with turbulent air conditions. Fog may seriously upset flying in the neighbourhood of airports, while falling rain, snow or hail may likewise reduce visibility.

Apart from these elements, visibility is affected by dust and smoke. Industrial areas and cities generally are obvious examples and since airports are situated locally, the reduction of visibility must be considered when airports are built. Forest and bush fires, e.g. in the Canadian prairies, reduce visibility to such an extent that visual contact with the ground from heights as low as 2,000–3,000 ft. may be negligible. Dust and blowing sand over deserts produce obscurity that may extend up to 10,000 ft. and reduce forward visibility to a mile.

A much-discussed problem concerns the formation of ice on the surfaces of aircraft under certain atmospheric conditions. If such ice is allowed to build up, the lifting capacity of the wings may be disastrously affected and engine performance may be so reduced as to constitute a power failure. Severe conditions producing such extremes are fortunately rare and modern aircraft in any case now carry de-icer systems for the flying surfaces, airscrews and cabin screens, while engine intakes and carburettors employ a heating device to the same end. Even so, prolonged flight under icing conditions can still reduce performance. Further, if the ice is to be successfully dispersed, immediate action is necessary as soon as the machine enters an icing zone. Most pilots take the precaution of using carburettor heating whenever icing is suspected. Modern turbine engines are not immune from icing, in fact under severe conditions they may be more prone than their reciprocating predecessors. Tests[6] on axial-flow turbo-jet and turbo-propeller engines indicated two problems. Unless sufficient heat is employed to disperse ice from the air intake and nose dome, ice may break off the lips of the intake and be swept into the engine. Provided the size of the ice splinter enables the ice to pass through the guide vanes and the ice is not brittle enough to shatter, a rotor blade may be bent, hit the guide vanes and result in the disintegration of the engine. Admittedly the possibility is remote, but enough heat must be available to obviate

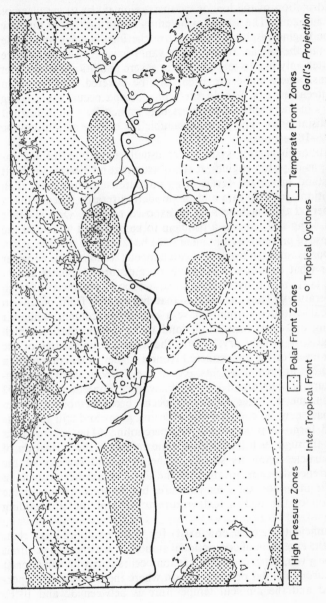

Figure 2 Weather regimes of the world (Summer in the Northern Hemisphere)

High Pressure Zones

—— Inter Tropical Front

Polar Front Zones

o Tropical Cyclones

Temperate Front Zones

Gall's Projection

the formation of the ice, or evasive action taken to get clear of the icing zone. The second problem is the restriction of air flow to the engine resulting from ice on the inlet screens and guide vanes of the engine. Intake guide vanes have been known to ice up after only five to ten minutes in severe conditions, while inlet screens, where these are used, can be covered over by ice in seventeen seconds. Should these phenomena occur, overheating occurs in the engine, and unless it is immediately shut down it will disintegrate. The period available for evasive action may be only 6–18 seconds.

Although heating systems are usually built into turbine engines, as in piston engines, it is still true that no aircraft yet built can stand prolonged severe icing conditions. Fortunately, such conditions are very rare and the modern aircraft's speed reduces the period the machine may be exposed to icing. On the other hand, icing still remains a problem to be reckoned with, and the expense of preventive equipment must be taken into consideration.

Our example showed what can happen; we must now consider under what conditions. Atmospheric moisture originates chiefly from evaporation over the oceans, a process enhanced by high temperatures. Thus air masses that have come from oceans in tropical latitudes normally have a high water content, while air flowing out from continental land masses, particularly in high latitudes, is usually dry. Again, the higher temperatures of the lower levels of the atmosphere favour a higher water content than is present at greater heights, e.g. at the Tropopause where temperature is approximately $-60°F.$, vapour content is only $0·02$ gm./cu. metre. Icing conditions occur because moisture in an air mass may be cooled below freezing point and still retain its liquid form—a process called 'supercooling'. The passage of a body through such an unstable zone results in the formation of ice particles upon its surfaces. The form and severity of the occurrence depends not only on the size of the water droplets in the air mass and their temperature, but to some extent on the relation of the body's temperature to that of the surrounding air.

Sufficient evidence now exists for us to be able to say that, with the exception of convectional clouds for which no lower limit can be given, dangerous ice accretion occurs only when an aircraft flies through cloud or freezing rain where the droplets are supercooled and the ambient temperature is between 32 and $10°F.$

Broadly speaking, the answer is to fly higher where temperatures are lower and the moisture is in the form of ice already, or fly lower where temperature is above the freezing point. One key to the incidence of icing conditions, therefore, is the height of the 'freezing level' over the area being considered. Finally we might note that, at true airspeeds in excess of 500 m.p.h., kinetic heating renders the aircraft immune from all but severe icing conditions.

Much research has been carried out with the aim of forecasting icing conditions, but the difficulties are great, since three parameters are involved, namely (*a*) cloud water content, (*b*) size of supercooled water droplet and (*c*) temperature. Of these three, the forecaster usually knows the last and then usually only the general distribution. In addition, it will be appreciated that supercooled water is unstable and any slight trigger action may change it to ice or snow. The only generality that can be made is that icing occurs in the narrow temperature band near the freezing point and is more severe in convection-type clouds. In a series of tests,[5] continuous icing was experienced when the water content was at least 0·305 gm./cu. metre with a droplet size of 13·7 microns and at an average temperature of −6·4°C.

Most people are aware of the importance of wind to aviation. The siting of airport runways will be dealt with at a later stage and we may here consider the effect of wind on aircraft in transit. Since the aeroplane is immersed in the atmosphere in flight, its speed may be calculated with reference either to the air surrounding it (airspeed) or with reference to the ground (ground speed). As far as the performance and safety of the machine is concerned, airspeed is the important element, but in calculating the time it would take to travel from one spot on the Earth's surface to another, ground speed is the relevant measurement. The difference between airspeed and ground speed will depend on the wind velocity. Thus, if the machine encounters a headwind of 20 m.p.h. and is travelling at a true airspeed of 200 m.p.h., its ground speed will be 180 m.p.h.

If we know the circulation of winds, we can begin to realize which routes are more likely to encounter headwinds or tailwinds and with what sort of frequency. It is well known that the eastbound crossing of the Atlantic is more favoured by tailwinds— the influence of the westerlies of temperate latitudes. Unfortunately, although most people are vaguely familiar with the surface wind pattern, not even the experts are sure of the wind

pattern at higher levels. With the development of modern transports using jet engines, the importance of a knowledge of
upper winds became vital and much research has already been
accomplished in this direction. Moreover, in order to preserve
economy of operation on long routes—particularly oceanic ones
—every effort must be made to take advantage of favourable
winds. On short stages, the navigator is justified in keeping to a
predetermined track, but with the birth of the long-range aircraft
and regular oceanic crossings, the aim became to make the
quickest possible crossing. The aim, within the limits of the aircraft's performance, was to calculate the 'least time track' between destinations, making use of all known or forecasted
favourable winds or 'least headwind' components. This method,
called 'pressure pattern' navigation, is now employed by all
transatlantic operators. It follows that a 'least time track' will
vary according to pressure and wind conditions and it is often
widely different from the great circle track—a modern example
of the old saying that the longest way round is the shortest way
home. It will be realized that, in order to follow the least time
track, the navigator does not keep to any predetermined
track.

As the performance of aircraft advanced, the altitudes at
which a machine could operate increased. Pressure-pattern
methods at these greater heights showed some surprising results.
It became clear that at heights around the 200–300 millibar
pressure level (about 28,000–40,000 ft. above sea level, temperate
regions, N. Hemisphere) fast-flowing streams of air existed, often
very narrow in extent and flowing from west–east over the Atlantic. Aircraft captains who 'rode' these streams made some
phenomenal crossing times. These streams—called 'jet streams'—
represent the most striking example of the differences between
surface and upper-wind conditions. The use of such streams
demands an accurate and up-to-the-minute knowledge of upper
air conditions, since jet streams are constantly in flux. From the
research that followed the realization of their possibilities, we
are beginning to understand the pattern of the upper atmosphere
for the first time. As yet, the picture is confused, and so rapid is
our increase of knowledge in this field that the picture changes
rapidly.

For our purposes, we only need a generalized map of the
upper winds so that we may compare them with the more familiar

surface pattern. It must be admitted that such a map can only be tentatively suggested (*Fig. 3*). In spite of the onrush of modern research, it must be remembered that few continuous observations of the upper atmosphere are available, and even then our knowledge over vast areas of the world is only fragmentary.

In *Fig. 3*, the circulation of winds at the 300-mb. pressure level is indicated, but the accuracy of the map deteriorates south of

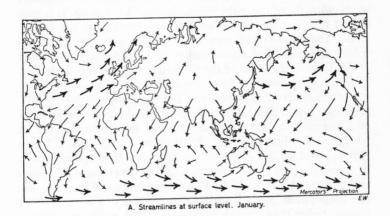

A. Streamlines at surface level. January.

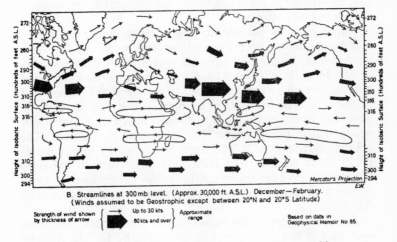

B. Streamlines at 300 mb. level. (Approx. 30,000 ft. A.S.L.) December—February.
(Winds assumed to be Geostrophic except between 20°N and 20°S Latitude)

Strength of wind shown by thickness of arrow { → Up to 30 kts. ➤ 80 kts and over } Approximate range

Based on data in Geophysical Memoir No 85.

Figure 3 Surface and upper winds of the world

about 20 degrees north where observations are scanty. The winds shown are assumed to obey the geostrophic relation except for the areas between the Tropics, which are separately calculated. The arrows indicate the Vector Mean Wind and at any given instant the actual wind may deviate from the values given, e.g. over the United Kingdom this deviation may be up to sixty knots.[2]

As an indication of modern knowledge on upper air conditions we may briefly consider the implications of jet streams. It is now almost certain that surface weather originates from the Tropopause. The latter is now seen as a very active part of the atmosphere and a marked accumulation of kinetic energy is found at this level in the zone of the westerlies. Such energy is derived from frontal action and from the absorption of solar energy by the ozone concentration near the Tropopause (30,000–40,000 ft. above sea level). The result is the creation of a fast-moving band of air around the globe in the region of the westerlies—the jet stream. The obstruction of the Western Cordillera of North America and of the Andes in the Southern Hemisphere, which lie across the path of the streams, results in the creation of vertical and horizontal waves which in turn create pulses of energy under the Tropopause. Such disturbances may give rise to several 'jet fingers' rather than a single flow. Again, such pulses may trigger new jet streams if other conditions are favourable, reforming a continuous wavy stream.

More generally, jet streams exist at frontal zones where they may be continuous or broken into several parts, and they flow west–east (although they have been recorded as flowing north–south). In width, they vary from forty to several hundred miles, but the more intensive examples are usually at the narrow end of the scale. The life cycle of an individual stream seems to be about two weeks, on the average, during which it tends to meander southwards in the Northern Hemisphere and lose altitude. The seasonal migration of frontal zones is reflected by similar movements in jet streams. The Himalayas, together with the steep temperature gradient between Asia and the Pacific, seem to speed up the jet stream and records show speeds up to 200 m.p.h. in this area.

Such, in outline, is the basis of upper atmospheric conditions —at least in temperate zones of the world. So far, the Atlantic routes are the chief examples where advantage is taken of these conditions; the modification of long transits in other parts of the world must await greater knowledge. Note, finally, that it is only the long routes that are affected and particularly those involving oceanic crossings.

From a discussion of the elements of weather, we may now turn to consider broader regional implications. In any study of air routes and their geographical position, the influence of weather must be considered in terms applicable to aviation. It is 'flying weather' that matters and of all the elements that are important, visibility and wind are the two most vital. 'Flying weather' is a term often used in aviation, but it is one that tends to mean different things to different persons. Thus a light plane, privately owned and used for pleasure and sport, is a different proposition from a transatlantic liner. The first operates almost entirely by reference to the ground—its instrumentation forbids otherwise—while the airliner must operate to a schedule carrying passengers in all kinds of weather and more often out of visual contact with the ground. The first machine flies by 'contact flying rules' or 'visual flight rules' (VFR), while the latter operates mostly under 'instrument flight rules' (IFR). The expressions 'fitness green' and 'fitness red' are used, indicating similar differences. The two categories imply definite weather minima beyond which aircraft may not operate. Such minima are laid down by international authority (I.C.A.O.) and implemented by national bodies. *Table 1* gives the general requirements for contact flying—i.e. flight and navigation by reference to the ground.

It follows that when conditions are below the minima given in the table, aircraft must either operate under IFR, or, if they are not equipped for prolonged flight on instruments alone, cease to operate until weather improves.

It will be seen that these rules take account of visibility only. As a basis for flying weather CFR and IFR lack important elements, although visibility alone can give insight into weather generally. *Figs. 4* and *5* show the percentage occurrence of contact flying weather for the British Isles and the USA on an annual basis. The stress on visibility is more important near airports where traffic is concentrated, and serves to remind us that take-off and landing are still the most vulnerable aspects of flight. When studying *Figs. 4* and *5* it should be remembered that the maps show general conditions and ignore local variations. An extension of these maps to include a wider proportion of the Earth's surface

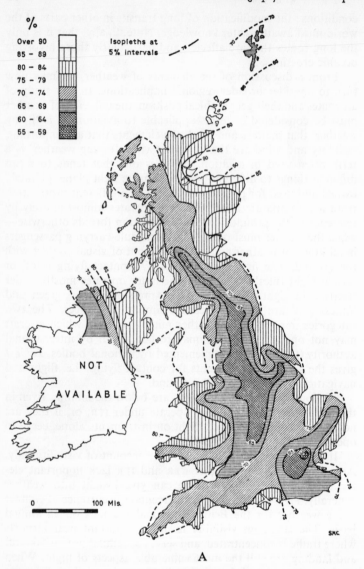

Figure 4 Flying weather in the British Isles. The maps show the percentage
A—day

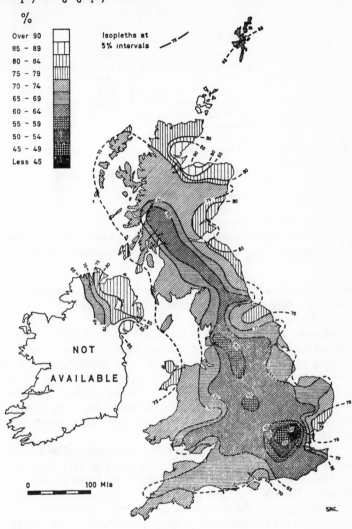

%

Over 90	
85 – 89	
80 – 84	
75 – 79	
70 – 74	
65 – 69	
60 – 64	
55 – 59	
50 – 54	
45 – 49	
Less 45	

Isopleths at
5% intervals

NOT

AVAILABLE

0   100 Mls

SMC.

B

occurrence of contact flying weather over a period of a year
  B—night

TABLE I

VISUAL FLIGHT RULES*

	(a) Within controlled airspace. (b) Outside controlled airspace at 200 metres (700ft.) or more above ground or water	(†a) Outside controlled airspace below 200 metres (700ft.) above ground or water
Flight Visibility Distance from Clouds	5 kms. (3 miles) 600 metres (2,000 ft.) horizontally 150 metres (500 ft.) vertically	1·5 kms. (1 mile) Clear of clouds

* *International Standards, Rules of the Air* (Second Edition), Annex 2. Convention on Civil Aviation
† Heights may be greater than these as individual states may specify. For UK see *A.N.O. 1954. Schedule II, Section IV*

would doubtless be useful, but we are once again up against the old problem—a lack of statistics. Even in the British Isles the position is not as good as it might be.

In order to broaden the basis of our maps of flying weather beyond that given in *Figs. 2–5*, we may make use of climatic data relating to temperature, pressure and wind. Such figures apply only to surface conditions and are of importance only in the vicinity of airports. Our ignorance of upper air conditions has already been noted when we dealt with winds, but those remarks apply equally to the related phenomena of temperature and pressure.

The prevalence of 'weather types' may be suggested by making use of all resources. This concept is not a new one. Gold[4] outlined a series of weather types for the British Isles based on pressure patterns. Bilham[1] has simplified Gold's work and suggested a more generally useful classification. The bases of such a classification are the characteristic pressure patterns observed over the British Isles over as long a period as records permit.

Bilham's results may be usefully compared with the maps in *Figs. 2–5*. In summary, his classification shows the variability of weather conditions in this country and it should be noted that extreme conditions of bad weather are absent. The prevalence of

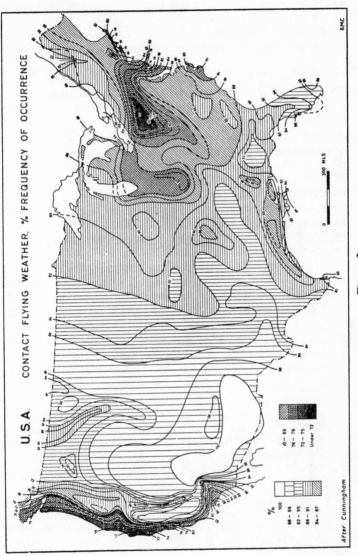

Figure 5

a westerly wind component and of cloud are important characteristics from our point of view.

The extension of the classification to the world as a whole
can be made only by an analysis of similar climatic data.

Weather and the turbo-jet airliner. An example[3]

The importance of meteorological conditions to the successful
operation of these aircraft may be seen by considering the effect
of temperature and wind changes on the range of the aircraft.
Assuming the aircraft takes off at the same weight and arrives
at its destination with an equivalent fuel reserve, then on a stage
of 1,500 nautical miles, a headwind component amounting to
50 knots reduces range by 170 nautical miles, while an increase in
temperature of 15°C. reduces range by 30 n.m.*

Provided the operation was carried out throughout at the
higher temperature, the fuel reserve at destination would be decreased by 4%. On the same basis, the 50-knot headwind would
reduce the reserve by 22%. In the latter case, in order to operate
at the same take-off weight and to arrive with the full fuel reserve
at the aircraft's destination, twelve or thirteen fewer passengers
could be carried. In the case of a temperature rise of 15°C., the
load would have to be reduced by two to three passengers only.

As with its piston-engined predecessors, the turbo-jet airliner
finds wind the most important element affecting its range and
payload.

REFERENCES

1. Bilham, E. G. *The Climate of the British Isles*. (London, 1938.)
2. Brooks, C. E. P., and others. *Upper Winds over the World*. Geophysical
   Memoir No. 85 (5th No. Vol. X), M.O. 499E, Meteorological Office,
   Air Ministry, 1950.
3. *Flight*, April 1952. 'Comet Flight Planning'.
4. Gold, E. *Aids to Forecasting*. Geogr. Memoir, Meteorological Office,
   Air Ministry, 1910.
5. Mason, D. 'Aircraft and Icing Research', *Weather*, August and September
   1953.
6. Thompson, J. K. 'Icing Problems for Turbojet and Turboprop Aircraft',
   Shell Aviation News, March 1956.

* The above figures relate to the De Havilland 'Comet' I airliner as
previously operated by *BOAC*.

3

THE TECHNICAL AND ECONOMIC
BACKGROUND

In the fifty years since the Wright brothers made their first powered flight, technical progress in aviation has been phenomenal. Much of this progress has been due to the demands of two world wars. In civil aviation, developments have not been so spectacular as in the military field, nor have they caught the public eye in the same way, but progress in reliability, safety and sheer economics has laid the foundation for modern air transport. Table II illustrates the progress that has been made and shows the essential characteristics of passenger-carrying machines of various dates from 1922 onwards. As far as possible these machines are representative of their period, but it should be borne in mind that there has been an increasing specialization of type since the more ubiquitous aeroplanes of the 1920's. The Bristol 'Britannia' is a long-range machine, but exists in several forms allowing for different stage lengths and passenger capacities. Such a specialized machine did not exist in the era of the D.H.50.

The significance of the figures given is best seen in terms of 'work capacity'. In aviation this capacity to do work is normally expressed as the ratio of load carried to the distance covered and the unit used is either the 'ton/mile' or 'passenger/mile'. Thus if one ton is carried one mile, the work done is 1 ton/mile. In order to ascertain the working capacity of the machines given in the example, one needs to know the number of hours the machines are flown over a certain period—usually a year. This 'utilization rate' was of the order of 1,000 hours a year in the 1920's or even lower—a reflection of market conditions and also the reliability,

TABLE II

HISTORICAL DEVELOPMENT OF AIRCRAFT PERFORMANCE

Year	Type	Seating capacity mail and freight	Cruising speed for a typical range. Still air. m.p.h. and statute miles
1922	De Havilland 34	8 passengers	105 m.p.h.—250 miles
1925	De Havilland 50	4 passengers and 200 lb. mail or freight	100 m.p.h.—375 miles
1928	Zeppelin LZ127* (airship)	Useful load = 20 passengers, 5 tons freight	70 m.p.h.—6,000 miles
1935	Zeppelin LZ129 (airship)	50 passengers and 10 tons freight	80 m.p.h.—8,000 miles
1935	Douglas DC–3	21 passengers	160 m.p.h.—800 miles
1938	Short S–23 'Empire' Flying Boat	17 passengers and 2 tons mail	160 m.p.h.—600 miles
1946	Douglas DC–4	44 passengers and mail and freight to All-up Wt. of 65,000 lb.	239 m.p.h.—1,750 miles
1952	De Havilland 'Comet' 1	36–40 passengers	500 m.p.h. (approx.) —1,500 miles
1957	Bristol 'Britannia' 300LR	65–120 passengers	350 m.p.h.—4,500 miles
1959	Douglas DC–8 Series 40	127–189 passengers	534 m.p.h.—6,110 miles
1959	Boeing 707–320	120–189 passengers	544 m.p.h.—4,625 miles
1964	1964 Vickers VC–10	115–151 passengers	547 m.p.h.—5,030 miles
1964	B.A.C. 111	65–79 passengers	539 m.p.h.—1,450 miles

* The load given assumes the use of hydrogen in the gasbags. The use of helium reduces the load by 7%

speed and range of the machine itself. Today, 3,000 hours is an average figure. For the purposes of calculation we will assume that each machine is utilized for the latter figure (3,000 hours each year), in order to provide a comparable base.

The capacity of the D.H.50 at 3,000 hours p.a. working at an average speed (i.e. including allowance for take-off and landings) of 80 m.p.h. would then be 1·9 million passenger/miles. At the more likely figure of 1,000 hours p.a., the capacity is 0·6 million passenger/miles. The later versions of the 'Britannia' working for 3,000 hours p.a. carrying 120 passengers and flying at an average net speed of 320 m.p.h. would accomplish 115 million passenger/ miles p.a. This difference may be appreciated when it is realized that the average annual capacity for a large airline at the present day is 3,200 million passenger/miles. Thus if 'Britannias' were used, a fleet of 28 could easily accomplish the work, whereas if the D.H.50 were employed, 1,690 machines would be required if used at 3,000 hours p.a., or over 5,000 if utilized at 1,000 hours p.a.! It should be remembered, of course, that a D.H.50 with spares would have cost about £5,000 in 1925, whereas the 'Britannia' with spares about £1,000,000 in 1956.

One further point might also be remembered, and that is that aircraft, like old soldiers, seldom wear out. Most aircraft become obsolete before their working life is complete, e.g. as the result of technical progress, but whereas the life of a machine on airline service was about 3–4 years on first-class routes in the 1920's, the cost of modern machines means that their life is usually some-what longer in service—about 5–10 years. Even so, this is still a high rate of turnover. In future this life may be extended still further, but when due allowance is made, the rate of technical progress is still likely to be formidable. All this progress has been achieved through the medium of one type of flying machine, and we must now consider its characteristics further, and also expand the field to include other possible types.

Flying machines may be divided into two broad categories. In the first place there are machines that gain lift by employing gasbags containing a gas lighter than air—hydrogen or helium— i.e. they are buoyant in the same way that a boat is buoyant on water. The net lift obtained is equal to the difference between the weight of the airship and the weight of air displaced. The machine will rise when its own weight is less than the weight of air it displaces and it will continue to do so until the two weights balance. Such machines, which include balloons and airships, are called 'aerostats'. Aerostats have the advantage of being able to remain motionless in the air and do not, therefore, require enormous runways. Very important, too, is the fact that the ratio of useful load available in terms of weight to the total all-up weight is the highest of all flying machines. For the Zeppelins of the inter-war years, the figure was 60% (*Table 2*). Nevertheless, the expense of providing a safe gas (helium) and the great volume required, together with their low speed, has not encouraged their development. The accidents—most of them avoidable, be it noted —that occurred in the inter-war years were chiefly responsible for their abandonment.

The second group obtain lift by making use of the resistance of the air to a moving body. When a suitably shaped surface— termed an aerofoil—is moved through the air at a slight angle, air resistance sets up forces that may be resolved into an upward, or lifting, component, and a backward or drag component. Machines using this principle, where the wings form the aerofoil, are called 'aerodynes'. The wing must be moved in relation to the surrounding air in order to create the pressure differences that give rise to lift and drag. This movement is provided by the engines which provide a thrust to pull the machine along and to resist the drag of the machine. In sailplanes gravity and moving air currents take the place of the engine.

There are two ways in which this principle may be applied. The vast majority of present-day aircraft have a fixed wing, and lift is obtained, therefore, by moving the whole machine. n the helicopter the wing is rotated, so that lift may be obtained without moving the whole aircraft through the air. It may be wondered why fixed-wing machines are ever used at all, but it should be remembered that helicopters have considerable limitations, particularly in forward speed, apart from which the control of the machine necessitates a formidable amount of 'revolving iron-mongery' which makes for a high first cost, and a high running cost. Lift may also be obtained by using a motor, usually a turbo-jet or better still a rocket, such that the thrust is greater than the machine's weight, as in the Hawker P.1127. So far such applications are of limited value, but some form of 'power take-off' in this manner, allied to a conventional fixed-wing configuration for normal flight, may yet make vast runways an anachronism.

Since the majority of current airliners are fixed-wing machines, we shall concentrate on their characteristics, but the foregoing discussion has tried to show that they may not remain supreme in their present form in the future. Should this be so, the pattern of airline operation may change. With fixed-wing aircraft the whole machine must be moved to obtain lift so that a field or runway is required upon which to gain flying speed, or, on landing, to lose it safely. Granted this, one might ask—but why a runway a mile or more long? The amount of lift required will depend on the weight of the aircraft. Thus the wing in flight must support the machine and each square foot of its area will carry a proportion of the weight. This is called 'wing loading' and is expressed in lbs./square foot. Putting it as simply as possible, lift depends on airspeed and the angle the wings make with the oncoming air stream, thus the more weight the wings are asked to lift, the greater the speed required to achieve and maintain flight, and the longer the runway needed for take-off and landing. Speed in flight is, in any case, sought after by the operator, since the utilization rate of the machine is affected by it. Speed requires power and with the advance in the power of the aero-engine came the progression sought after, but at the price of higher wing loadings. Small wonder that the 7–10 lbs./square foot wing loading of the 1920's has given place, e.g. to the Boeing 707's wing loading of up to 110 lbs./square foot. The result has been an upward progression in the length of take-off and landing run, which for the Boeing 707–320 can reach up to 10,000 feet at sea level in temperate latitudes. The enormous fabric of London Airport or Kennedy, New York, is an essential part of the picture. What is debatable is how much longer we can afford to allow airports to grow, for the problems of alternative land-use become more formidable with each new airport. Also they recede further and further from the city centres they are supposed to serve.

Like all carriers, the aeroplane exists to transport a quantity of goods or passengers from one point to another, but unlike all other forms of transport, it lifts this weight into the air and must sustain it there until its destination is reached. This latter feature involves a considerable expenditure of effort, and weight, therefore, is a critical consideration. The loaded weight of the machine may be broken down into three principal parts: the weight of the machine in working trim, less fuel, i.e. its tare weight; the weight of the crew and their equipment, which for all intents and purposes is a constant also; and finally the weight represented by the fuel and cargo—the disposable load. The cargo (or passengers) represents the revenue-earning load and is called the payload.

A choice is therefore possible, since one may carry either a heavy fuel load and a small payload over a long distance or vice versa. This is represented hypothetically in *Fig. 6* and is an im-

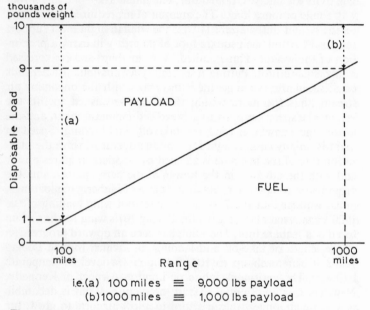

i.e. (a) 100 miles ≡ 9,000 lbs payload
    (b) 1000 miles ≡ 1,000 lbs payload

Figure 6 Diagram to show the relationship between fuel and payload
(Hypothetical figures)

portant result. A comparison of the figures in that table with the corresponding figures for any other form of transport would show that the tare weight of the aircraft represents a very high proportion of the total 'all-up' weight. Having read this far, the reader should by now have some idea of why this should be so.

The aeroplane is thus seen as a highly specialized piece of machinery involving high costs of maintenance to keep it in trim, and able to carry only a small payload in relation to its total weight and power. In addition, the rate of technical progress imposes a high rate of obsolescence. In return it offers an unparalleled freedom of movement at high speed. Where this is important the machine is unmatched by any other transport form.

Some more general points should be noted to conclude the technical discussion. In the first place the stability and control characteristics of the aeroplane make it essential that the centre of gravity should be kept within well-defined limits. This means that for cargo machines in particular, very careful loading is necessary and this places restriction on certain very bulky loads. Closely allied to this aspect of load suitability is the question of the size and shape of the aircraft fuselage in which the payload is carried. In fast modern airliners the space available is long and tube-like, which, while not restricting passenger-loading, can and does make freight carriage difficult. Since the war the specialized freighter has put in an appearance. This is normally not a high-performance machine, but one with easy loading facilities—e.g. nose or tail doors (unlike the awkward side doors on older machines)—slung low above the ground so that freight may be loaded straight off a lorry or landing-stage, and with a square-shaped hold better able to cope with the multifarious shapes usual with cargo units. In addition these machines have a more generous range of movement for the centre of gravity of the loaded vehicle. Speed is not the prime consideration, since even a modest cruising speed of 150 m.p.h. is far above that of a cargo ship, train or motor vehicle. In any case, the bulbous square shape would prohibit high speeds unless an inordinate amount of power were available. For the high-speed liner carrying passengers and mail only, close attention to streamlining is essential to reduce the form drag of the structure in flight, and this normally leaves the interior space as the familiar 'tube'. Pressurization of the internal space to enable passengers to be carried at high altitudes, without the need for individual oxygen equipment or pressure suits, also favours a fuselage of either circular or 'double-bubble' cross-section. Finally, it should be noted that the aeroplane represents a flexible 'unit' type vehicle. That is to say, it carries its own power supply and operates as a relatively small individual unit. In this sense it resembles the motor-coach or truck, and contrasts with the bulk carriers exemplified by the railways.

In economic terms the costs involved in air transport may be divided into 'fixed' costs which are incurred whether the machines operate or not, and the 'variable' or 'operational' costs

Other terms have been used, but they indicate a similar division. Thus in the USA the terms 'direct' and 'indirect' are more often employed, while occasionally the term 'flight' costs is used for variable costs. The units employed in the evaluation of cost vary with the purpose of the costing account. For our purposes fixed costs may be considered in terms of a month or a year, while variable costs will be expressed as so much per aircraft hour (A/hr.). The time unit in the latter case refers to actual operational time on the part of the aircraft. Total cost will then include both categories and each machine must bear a proportion of the fixed costs as well as its operational expenses. This figure may also be expressed in terms of A/hr.

The allocation of particular items to one or other of the main categories varies between different authorities, and it must be admitted that some items are composite in character—e.g. a pilot's salary is normally calculated on an annual basis and is paid whether he flies or not. Such expenditure is a fixed cost, but where a bonus is given for so many hours flown in addition, this represents a variable commitment. Other items are marginal cases and this should be borne in mind while one is considering this subject.

Fixed costs include not only the costs of ground installations, offices, salaries, insurance, advertising, etc., but also the capital depreciation on the aircraft fleet. This latter item is a large one (from 3–17% of total cost p.a.) since, as we have seen, machines are normally written off in a short period, e.g. 7–10 years in the USA, slightly longer in Europe. The salaries of the aircrew will normally be considered as fixed cost also. A proportion of these costs must be borne by each working aircraft and it will be seen that the more work the machines do, the more the cost load may be spread ; in other words, a high 'utilization rate' is advantageous. There are limits to the rate that can be achieved, thus faster aircraft can do more work in a given time, while long routes favour a higher rate than shorter ones. On the long international routes a utilization rate of 3,500 hours p.a. is possible, while on medium- and short-range work the figure is nearer 1,500–2,500 hours p.a. Nevertheless, the point is an important one, and undoubtedly the phenomenal increase in aircraft cruising speeds since 1919 is a reflection of the need.

Operating costs are incurred only when the machines are operating. Since they depend on hours flown, the calculation is made in terms of cost per A/hr. The maintenance and repair of aircraft is a big item normally considered under variable costs, but even if a machine is not flying some maintenance is necessary, partly because of legally enforced airworthiness requirements and partly because it is a highly complex machine that is best kept in trim for as much of the time as possible. Again, good maintenance is essential if a high utilization rate is aimed at, and indeed the whole struggle for increased speed has meant a corresponding increase in maintenance costs. Maintenance represents about 10% of total costs and may equal up to 40% of the original capital investment each year. That this is a high figure is well seen when it is realized that for an ocean steamer maintenance represents an annual expenditure equal to only 2% of the original investment. The other large item is fuel cost, and we have already seen why this will always tend to be a big item. Attempts to reduce the consumption per mile have so far been at the expense of either performance, or increased maintenance, or both. Besides fuel, other items like landing fees are included in the variable cost category. Costs that are incurred at each take-off and landing, such as landing fees, are very important where the operator is working short distances, since a higher proportion of the aircraft's time is spent in taking-off and landing. Indeed, one authority[1] places them in a category of their own.

It will be realized that operating costs must vary with the type of aircraft used and the distances it flies. Particular aircraft may be more suited to short-range than long-range work. In other words, for each aircraft type there will be a distance over which it is most economic to operate, and this is normally the maximum distance or sector it can cover non-stop with full load. If it is operated beyond this distance it must sacrifice load for fuel, while below it, landing costs will increase and its speed from runway to runway (block speed) will be reduced.

Strictly speaking, no fixed-wing aircraft is economic below a sector distance of about 180–200 miles. *Table III* illustrates the economic sector distance idea with reference to the 'Viscount' airliner operated by British European Airways. Before studying the table, one other variable must be introduced. It is of little use operating the aircraft if there is no market for its services. Thus 'load factor' is important—i.e. the proportion of seats/freight capacity actually sold to the maximum capacity offered. This is sometimes called the 'achieved load factor'. When considering

TABLE III

VICKERS 'VISCOUNT' V-701 OPERATIONS

	Sector Distances (statute miles)		
	200	600	1,000
Maximum payload (lb.)	11,808	11,808	11,450
Block speed (m.p.h.)	150	245	270
Time for distance (hours)	1·33	2·45	3·7
Cost per aircraft/mile (sh.)	18·6	10·5	8·86
Cost per seat/mile (pence)	4·75	2·69	2·26
No. of passengers required to break even on Total Costs (Thousand £)	28·4	18·3	16·6
Total Revenue per annum per aircraft at 65% load factor (Thousand £)	285	464	516
Total cost per annum per aircraft (Thousand £)	265	276	280
NET PROFITABILITY PER ANNUM PER AIRCRAFT (Thousand £)	20	188	6

Source: P. G. Masefield, *Progress in British Air Transport*

load factor from the point of view of costs, there will be a minimum average load that the aircraft must carry for the operator to break even. The 'break-even' load factor will vary with the aircraft type and the cost structure involved in its operation. Capital Airlines gave 52% as the break-even load factor for their 'Viscounts', while they achieved a figure as high as 82%. British European Airways achieved a figure nearer 65%, probably due to their shorter sector distances.

Before considering markets, two points may be emphasized. Firstly, costs are related to hours flown by the machine, whereas its revenue earning capacity will depend on the number of revenue miles it can cover. Thus the faster the aircraft, and the more miles flown, the greater its revenue earning capacity will be. In other words its utilization is more effective, and this is the reason why the fast, but expensive, turbo-jet airliner can be successfully operated.

Tables IV and *V* illustrate some further aspects of cost analysis and should be used in addition to *Table III*.

TABLE IV

PERCENTAGE BREAKDOWN OF EXPENDITURE IN AIRLINE OPERATIONS:
BRITISH EUROPEAN AIRWAYS

Item	Year 1954–55 %	Year 1963–64 %
Amortization of fleet	6·7	11
Pay, allowances and pensions	42·8	39
Fuel and oil	11·8	8
Fuel tax	2·3	
Commission	6·3	7
Accommodation	3·5	3
Sales and publicity	2·2	
Landing fees	3·5	6
Aircraft maintenance	9·1	7
Passenger meals		3
Other costs	7·6	4
Interest	3·8	7
Profit	0·4	5
	100·0	100

Source: *BEA Report and Accounts, 1954–55* and *1963–64*

Before discussing the market for air services, we must first remind ourselves of the volumetric and weight restrictions inherent in the aircraft. Unlike their surface counterparts, aircraft do not yet show anything like the same degree of specialization according to function. The cargo aircraft is essentially similar to its passenger-carrying relative, and in many cases the same airframe is used, e.g. the Douglas DC–6A all-cargo machine and its counterpart on passenger service, the DC–6B. Machines like the DC–6B have space for mail and cargo as well as for passengers—a characteristic of most so-called 'passenger' machines. This mixed nature is of fundamental importance as we shall see later. Since 1945, specialization has begun and it is not difficult to distinguish between such extremes as the long-range transatlantic airliner and the heavy duty freighter, e.g. compare the Boeing 707 with the Short & Harland 'Belfast' freighter. Yet even here mixed cargo and passenger loads can be carried. It would be interesting to see passenger reaction if the rolling stock for the 'Flying Scotsman' appeared one day as twelve or more coal wagons! *Table VI* suggests the degree of specialization that has emerged so far.

TABLE V

UTILIZATION RATE AND AIRCRAFT COSTS: AN EXAMPLE

Assumptions made for the purpose of the example:
Fleet of 1 aircraft. Maximum payload 3 tons at average block speed of 250 m.p.h.
Total fixed cost—£6,000 p.a.
Operating costs—£17 A/hr.

A. Utilization of 100 hours per month. 12 months' operation a year

On an hourly basis—Fixed cost per machine	£5
Operating cost	£17
Total	£22

At full capacity (*load factor 100%*)—3 tons is carried 250 miles in one hour at a cost of £22
= 7d. per ton/ml. (approx.)   1
At *load factor of 50%*
= 14d. per ton/ml.   2

B. Utilization of 200 hours per month. 12 months' operation p.a.

On an hourly basis—Fixed cost	£2·5
Operational costs	£17
Total	£19·5

At *load factor of 100%*
= 6d. per ton/ml.   3
At *load factor of 50%*
= 12d. per ton/ml.   4

Now a shipper of cargo from London–Delhi, a distance of 5,550 miles, would pay at the following rates:

Case A—Cost rates: From 1 above   £162 per ton shipped
From 2 above   £324 per ton shipped
Case B may be considered in a similar way.

Air transport is a high-cost medium, as has already been suggested, but in order to appreciate this fact, comparison with alternative modes of transport is necessary. For passenger work, the average cost per mile to the passenger on scheduled airlines averages 2·5d.–15d., whereas railway rates average 1d.–3·5d. and shipping rates on tourist service about the same. Such rates apply to European conditions and are not typical of the world as a whole. For freighting, the position is not so easy to assess, but for long-range ocean traffic it is estimated[2] that by sea the average rate is £10 per ton, compared with £500–£1,000 per ton

TABLE VI

AIRCRAFT SPECIALIZATION

Type	Characteristics (Cruising speed) m.p.h.)	Approximate economic sector distance (miles)*
Long-range airliner e.g. Boeing 707–320	4 engines 544 m.p.h.	4,625
Medium range e.g. Viscount 800	4 engines 305 m.p.h.	1,290
Trident	3 engines 577 m.p.h.	2,035
BAC 111	2 engines 539 m.p.h.	1,450
Short-range and 'Feederliners' e.g. Hawker Siddeley 748	2 engines 276 m.p.h.	1,105
Herald 200	2 engines 274 m.p.h.	1,110
Specialized Freighter e.g. Argosy (Series 220)	4 engines 277 m.p.h.	945
Helicopters e. g. Bristol 171 Mark IIIA	1 engine 90 m.p.h.	59
Sikorsky S.61 N	2 engines 148 m.p.h.	85

*Maximum payload
Source: *Flight International*

by air. In terms of ton/miles, freight rates for the United States internal network average 10*d.* ton/ml., for the U.S. Transatlantic services 2*s.* 11*d.* ton/ml., and for other long-range operators 3*s.* 6*d.* ton/ml.

When such comparisons have been made an important proviso must be added. Costs per ton/mile in air transport (with the possible exception of passenger traffic) are 'high' in comparison with surface transport, but the availability of surface links is not the same in any two areas. What may be true for the dense sea network of the North Atlantic, or the road and rail networks of Western Europe and the United States, is certainly not true for the bulk of the southern continents or most of Asia. It is necessary, therefore, to bear in mind the alternatives when considering any particular region.

The aeroplane relies much on speed for its market appeal, i.e. a saving of time and distance. As important is its flexibility conferred upon it by the fact that it needs no track or road and it is, therefore, immune from the grosser physical barriers. The bottleneck in this respect is the airport—still the 'Achilles heel' of aviation, particularly where the operation of large transports is concerned. The price paid for speed and flexibility is the high power/weight ratio required, which in turn means a modest payload. The advantages to be derived in terms of time depend to a large extent on the length of the journey. Modern international airports being what they are, the passenger has to make a ground journey from city centre to the outlying airport. On short routes this ground time may occupy as much as 50% of the total travelling time. The air journey hardly gains over surface transport in this case, no matter how fast the aircraft may be, e.g. *Table VII*.

TABLE VII

AIR JOURNEY LONDON–PARIS

Journey speed from London (city centre)–Paris (city centre):		
1921 Overall average speed	=	53 m.p.h.
Aircraft's cruising speed		80 m.p.h.
1951 Overall average speed	=	71 m.p.h.
Aircraft's cruising speed		165 m.p.h.
Percentage increase in overall speed	=	35%
Percentage increase in aircraft speed	=	106%
See also TABLE LIV		

On long trunk routes the ground time shrinks to an insignificant fraction of the total. The elimination of lengthy ground journeys is currently occupying the minds of airline companies and airport authorities, and many ideas have been suggested to overcome it.* For freight traffic, speed is still important, but is

* See also Chapter 8.

not the exclusive element, except for perishable or urgently required commodities. Lighter packing requirements, less vibration,
less pilferage and lower insurance rates, together with fewer
transhipments, all play a part. Such considerations suggest that
air transport will be both competitive and complementary to the
older forms.

We may now tackle the central question—what is the nature
of air traffic and where is it generated? As a first step, let us consider some 'sample' cargoes and their possibilities as air cargo,
before considering the actual pattern.

(a) Passenger.
(b) Iron ore.
(c) Radio valves.
(d) Potatoes.
(e) 12-day budding roses.
(f) A ship's propeller.

(a) The passenger represents a 'cargo' where speed is an important element. The passenger travelling on business is enabled
to contact personally, and with less fatigue, a much wider range
of customers. Air travel cuts out a proportion of hostelry expenses
that would be incurred if he had travelled by slower surface
transport. For the tourist, similar considerations apply, only this
time a wider range of resorts, or places of interest, replace the
customer of the business man. For the airline operator, a number
of important factors must be considered. Passengers require a
good deal of space, pleasant surroundings, and they must be fed
and looked after. It follows, therefore, that the longer the time
taken on the journey, the more important these elements loom
in the operator's expense sheet. This question of space available,
and time, operates against the bulk carriers. One has only to
compare the railway carriage and the coal truck to realize which
is likely to 'pack more revenue' for the railway authorities.
Passengers, therefore, incur higher costs in surface transport in
comparison with cargo traffic, with the result that air transport
reaps a decided advantage. Indeed, passenger fares on all forms
of transport are very similar, especially on distances over 200
miles.

Two other elements are important. In the first place the
passenger virtually loads and unloads himself—an advantage to

the air operator where time is money. Secondly, the passenger usually returns from his travels, i.e. the traffic is 'two-way'. Unfortunately, as *Table VIII* shows, although over a year there may be a balance of departures and arrivals, there is usually a seasonal aspect to the movements when shorter time periods are taken. This means that for the operator there is a problem of 'return' loading at most seasons of the year. Freight is essentially 'one way' by its very nature, and there need not be any annual balance of traffic over the routes concerned.

We have noted, previously, that specialization in aircraft is

TABLE VIII

PASSENGER TRAFFIC MOVEMENTS

(*A*) Total Annual Movements—United Kingdom:

	(*thousands*) 1962	
	By sea	By air
Passengers arriving in the UK	3,692	3,866
Passengers departing from the UK	3,671	3,809

(*B*) Seasonal Movements:

	Transatlantic Passenger Traffic 1963	
Passengers carried all classes	Airline (*scheduled*)	Steamship
(*a*) Eastbound:		
1st quarter	188,890	36,667
2nd quarter	355,933	144,265
3rd quarter	378,078	150,992
4th quarter	230,880	57,326
Total	1,153,781	389,250
(*b*) Westbound:		
1st quarter	191,047	41,247
2nd quarter	258,897	118,336
3rd quarter	524,110	158,152
4th quarter	294,432	81,387
Total	1,268,486	399,122

Sources: (A) *Annual Abstract of Statistics*. HMSO
       (B) *Tourism in O.E.C.D. Member Countries*. *World Air Transport Statistics*, I.A.T.A.

not well marked. Further, the payload capacity is relatively small, with the result that the passenger machine is not markedly different in size or layout from the cargo carrier. Indeed, most machines carry both. The savings in space resulting from the removal of furnishings and galleys, etc., do not provide a notable increase in cargo space in an aircraft over and above that available in a passenger machine. The opposite is true for the bulk carrier. In terms of costs, cargo rates are little different from passenger rates in air transport—a distinctive feature.

In summary, the passenger represents a very suitable cargo for the air operator and accounts for the greatest proportion of his revenue.

(b) Iron ore represents a basic raw material required by modern industry. It is bulky and anything up to 80% of its weight may be represented by useless 'gangue'. It is, therefore, of low value per unit weight, and is unable to stand high costs of transport. The demand for ore is a continuous one so that a continuous stream of supplies must be forthcoming. Furthermore, that stream must be a weighty one, since quantity is also important. Such a cargo is an excellent example of a 'pipeline' commodity, i.e. a continuous stream or pipeline of supply is needed. This can be met by a fleet of vehicles each arriving one after the other and forming a chain. It will be seen that, once the chain has been started, speed is of relatively little importance provided there are enough vehicles. Note, however, that much stock is locked-up in transit. Here, then, is a cargo completely alien to the economic and technical characteristics of the aeroplane, but admirably suited to the bulk carrier, particularly the ship.

(c) Radio valves represent an intricate and delicate product of highly specialized industry. Only a small proportion of its value is represented by the raw materials embodied in its manufacture. By far the greater proportion of its value is added by manufacture —mostly by skilled labour. It has, therefore, considerable value in relation to unit weight and, in addition, it is as well to remember its fragility. Unlike iron ore, valves are not wanted continuously, i.e. a pipeline has no value here. The buyer expects regular shipments at intervals that he specifies and he does not want half of the valves to be broken by the time they reach him. Such goods can stand relatively high transport costs (like many similar small products of industry) and we would expect air transport to prove a suitable medium.

(*d*) Potatoes may be considered the agricultural homologue of iron ore. Bulky, and of low unit value, they are essential commodities in temperate countries at least. Supplies must be continuous, as with iron ore, unless extensive stock-piling is possible. There are differences, however. Potatoes are not nearly so homogeneous as some may think. At the beginning of the season, new potatoes can command a high price and the first supplier reaps the benefit. Speed becomes important here, and for a short period potatoes might even stand the high costs of air transport.

(*e*) Rosebuds represent another agricultural commodity, but this time more akin to the radio valve in characteristics. Small in bulk, highly perishable and incorporating a considerable measure of value 'added by manufacture', if one may put it that way, the rosebud seems eminently suitable as an air cargo. Furthermore, its market area is strictly controlled by the fact that after twelve days it becomes useless. Thus British examples that used to sell only as far afield as the European continent when surface transport was employed, may now be sold as far afield as the South American countries. Supply is highly seasonal, since climatic circumstances are relevant, with the result that shipments will be neither continuous nor necessarily regular. In short, rosebuds represent a cargo that is light in weight, perishable and much affected by speed of shipment, so that the aircraft seems well able to cater for its needs.

(*f*) Like the radio valve, a ship's propeller is a product of highly skilled industry, but this time each unit is of considerable weight. Propellers do not often enter into the transport world as cargo, for obvious reasons, but when they do, the circumstances are interesting. Normally, one would not expect to find a ship's propeller on an aircraft's load manifest, but there is one exception. Under emergency conditions it may pay to fly a propeller out to a disabled ship, rather than allow the ship to remain idle until a new propeller can be brought out by sea. Speed has become an important element, and costs must be viewed in the light of the emergency.

In other words, the ship's propeller may be taken as an example of an 'emergency' cargo, and it serves to remind us of the importance of prevailing conditions when discussing transport.

From a consideration of our sample cargoes, we may make a first approximation of the requirements of air traffic. In summary —the following conditions seem relevant:

(a) The nature of the commodity—value per unit weight, perishability, etc. Demand for it—pipeline characteristics, etc.

(b) Time and distance.

(c) Density of alternative surface networks.

Having considered the position theoretically, we may now confront our findings with reality. *Tables IX–XV* give an idea of the position. *Table IX* illustrates the relationship of transport

TABLE IX

THE RELATIONSHIP OF TRANSPORT FORMS—UNITED KINGDOM

	Passenger (000's million pass.-mls.)			Freight (000's million ton-mls.)		
	1952	1958	1961	1952	1958	1961
Rail	24·0	22·1	21·0	22·4	18·3	17·6
Road: Public	50·1	43·4	43·9 ⎱	18·8	23·1	27·9
Private	37·4	67·6	77·7 ⎰			
Air: Domestic Scheduled	0.12	0·3	0·6	0·001	0·002	0·004

Note: That the load carried in terms of weight (1961) was:
Rail: freight 89%
passenger 11%
Air: freight 8%
passenger 92%

Sources: *Annual Abstracts of Statistics*
BTC Reports
British Road Fedn. Basic Road Statistics
British Railway Board Reports

forms in the United Kingdom and illustrates the point that passenger traffic is by far the most important source of revenue for air transport. Railways and shipping depend far more on freight for their bread and butter. In the field of passenger traffic, we would expect air transport to be competitive with surface alternatives. Much depends on the length of the route, as we have already suggested. *Table X* shows the picture for the long-distance Atlantic routes and it will be seen that the aeroplanes' position is very strong. Indeed, except for the specialized 'sea

TABLE X

ATLANTIC PASSENGER TRAFFIC 1948–63

Year	Air Passengers (thousands) % in parentheses	Sea Passengers (thousands) % in parentheses	Total (thousands)
1948	253 (28)	637 (72)	890
1949	273 (29)	672 (71)	945
1950	317 (29)	762 (71)	1,079
1951	339 (32)	710 (68)	1,049
1952	446 (35)	844 (65)	1,290
1953	510 (36)	900 (64)	1,410
1963	2,836 (78)	788 (22)	3,624

Sources: 'The Recent Development of Passenger Air Transport'.
Lecture at Fourteenth Congress of International
Chamber of Commerce, by S. Tomasino
I.A.T.A., World Air Transport Statistics
Tourism in O.E.D.C. Member Countries

cruise' where time is no object, the aeroplane now carries the bulk
of the Atlantic passenger traffic. *Table XI* illustrates another
development—the introduction of tourist-class services in air
transport. This is a normal development that has its analogues in
shipping and railway practice, but has undoubtedly been responsible for much of the recent increase in air-passenger traffic on
the Atlantic, as well as on other routes. Over the shorter distances,
railway and road transport are in a stronger position. Competi-

TABLE XI

RELATIVE GROWTH OF TOURIST TRAFFIC
(BOAC Scheduled Services)

Year	First-Class Passengers %	Tourist/Economy Class %
1952–53	86·5	13·5
1953–54	67·5	32·5
1954–55	54·8	45·2
1963–64	10·0	90·0

Source: *BOAC*

tion on routes of less than 200 miles must await the coming of a practical helicopter.

In the sphere of freight traffic, *Tables XII* and *XIII* show

TABLE XII

IMPORTS AND EXPORTS THROUGH AIRPORTS:
UNITED KINGDOM 1963

Item	Imports (c.i.f.) £ millions	Exports (f.o.b.) £ millions
Live animals	3·8	3·6
Hides, skins, furs	10·8	0·6
Metalliferous ores and scrap	6·3	—
Chemical elements and compounds	4·9	1·4
Medicines and pharmaceutical products	1·9	10·0
Leather, leather goods and dressed furs	3·0	4·4
Textile yarn, fabrics and made-up articles	19·8	10·7
Non-ferrous metals	2·0	10·3
Manufactures of metal	3·3	3·0
Machinery other than electric	52·9	63·1
Electric machinery, apparatus and appliances	32·2	30·1
Transport equipment and parts	9·6	24·4
Clothing	16·4	10·2
Footwear	4·9	—
Professional and scientific instruments, photographic and optical goods, watches and clocks	19·1	17·5
Miscellaneous manufactured articles	24·1	21·7
Rubber manufactures	—	0·9
All other goods	11·3	23·2
	226·5	235·0

Source: *Board of Trade Journal*

typical conditions for operators in the United Kingdom and the USA. *Table XIV* shows a somewhat different picture, for here we are dealing with a route that is poorly served by surface transport. The lesson is, I think, sufficiently obvious to need no further comment here.

One final feature of market conditions concerns seasonal variations. Annual figures, such as those given in the tables so far, mask such changes in traffic intensity. Passenger traffic is

TABLE XIII

IMPORTS AND EXPORTS THROUGH AIRPORTS:
UNITED STATES (March 1960)

(Principal Commodities with Shipping Weights over 150,000 lb.)

Commodities	Shipping Weight (lb.)
Exports	
Hatching eggs	430,321
Refrigerators, electric, household	424,578
Kitchen and tableware, plastic	415,232
Automobile equipment and parts	411,877
Television sets	289,954
Cut flowers and cut ferns or foliage	231,450
Tracklaying tractor parts	210,206
Baby chicks	155,425
Engine parts, internal combustion	153,012
Total all commodities	12,855,390
Imports	
Beef, fresh, chilled or frozen, boneless	1,159,068
Shrimps and prawns	609,229
Fresh cucumbers	594,677
Automobile parts	507,280
Beef, fresh, chilled or frozen, bone in	431,389
Wool fabrics	393,400
Coffee essenced, substitutes, adulterants	271,008
Okra, fresh	219,401
United States miscellaneous articles returned	188,719
Tomatoes	188,252
Peppers, fresh	188,851
Total all commodities	8,536,698

Source: *Air Transportation*, November 1960

particularly susceptible to this sort of rhythm, e.g. tourist traffic is more concentrated in the summer season on the Atlantic route, but in the winter season between New York and Miami. *Table XV* illustrates seasonal fluctuations on British European Airways' network. Freight is not affected in quite the same way, but early fruit and vegetable traffic—as our 'new potato' example suggested —shows a marked seasonal trend.

TABLE XIV

A. SAMPLE FREIGHT LIST, SEATTLE–JUNEAU (ALASKA)
(Inbound to Juneau)

Fresh fruit	690 lb.
Fried potatoes	68 lb.
Fresh meat	1,000 lb.
Plate glass	2,000 lb.
Barber's chairs	6
Light tractor	1

Miscellaneous—including: metal sheets, military stores, mining machinery spares, one hamster and a canary. Laundry.*

B. GROWTH OF AIR FREIGHT TRAFFIC: SEATTLE–ALASKA
(Inbound traffic to Juneau for a typical company)

Year Peak month's traffic	Freight lb.
1940	1,704
1947	30,000
1948	160,000
1950	250,000
1954	600,000 (estimated)

Source: 'Alaska's Airlines', *Flight*, February 1952

* Laundry for Fairbanks and Juneau customers is carried out in Seattle at the rate of 30 cents/lb., including delivery on the 3,400-mile round trip. This rate is only slightly higher than the laundry service at Fairbanks itself

TABLE XV

REVENUE PASSENGER TRAFFIC 1963–64:
BRITISH EUROPEAN AIRWAYS MONTHLY TOTALS

Month	Total Revenue Passengers Carried (All routes)
April 1963	461,938
May	490,256
June	565,117
July	657,918
August	691,598
September	632,036
October	462,436
November	310,734
December	324,416
January 1964	310,403
February	297,310
March	400,650

Source: *BEA Report and Accounts 1963–64*

This brings us to the end of our discussion on the origin of air traffic and we may now consider the geographical distribution of the market. The burden of the next chapter will be to consider the world plan of air routes, but we may first draw some general conclusions concerning the 'where' of air transport as a result of our findings in the last few chapters.

Two things appear to be essential for the development of a dense net of airways. Firstly, a dense population may provide the source of passenger traffic on a large scale. But population density is manifestly insufficient, since many areas with a dense population, e.g. China or India, do not give rise to heavy air traffic. Such a region must also be economically advanced—a concept we shall consider later. In particular, a marked development of manufacturing industry appears to be essential. The prime examples here are Western Europe and the United States. The political factor has not as yet bothered us, but a glance at a map reveals that this aspect cannot be neglected in a study of air patterns. To realize that international air transport operates mainly through 295 bilateral agreements between states is but to touch the fringe of the problem. Then, finally, one must consider the relative importance of air transport in a region. Thus although air traffic is quantitatively small in under-developed territories, it may still be of vital importance to that territory because of the poor state of surface transport. Thus the total freight traffic carried by air in Northern Canada may not reach the proportions of traffic further south in the same continent, but the relative importance of air freight in Northern Canada is very great, since surface links are so sparsely developed. In such regions the aircraft becomes the pioneer—perhaps the most exciting aspect of all commercial aviation.

REFERENCES

1. Masefield, P. G. 'Recent Progress in British Air Transport', *Advancement of Science*, Volume XII, No. 47, 1955.
2. *The Financial Times*, 7th September, 1953.
3. Slater, John E. 'Transatlantic air and sea travel: an analysis of the effect of the first ten years of post-war scheduled air service over a major intercontinental route', *International Air Transport Association*, Bulletin 21, p. 29, 1955.
4. World Air Transport Statistics. *International Air Transport Association*, Annual.

Part Two

4

WORLD AIR ROUTES

The discussion so far has tried to make clear the possibilities of commercial aviation, and the way is now open for a consideration of actual or potential operations. Before considering the major air routes, we may briefly summarize the position reached so far.

Physically, aircraft are by no means so free as is sometimes imagined. All operations begin and terminate on the ground, while in the air the machines are guided by ground-located radio aids. For these reasons, the importance of topographical considerations should not be forgotten beside the more obvious claims of the weather. Economically, aircraft exist to supply a transport service so that the location of markets for that service are important. No matter how attractive a route may appear on a map, it will fail to establish itself if no one wants to use it. Historically the aeroplane arrived late upon the scene and has usually had to face up to a world long bound by surface links, i.e. the aircraft's major sources of custom are already fixed. This does not mean that no alteration in the pattern is possible; it simply represents a geographical fact. Politically, too, the 'ground plan' is surface orientated. One has only to consider the crowded national states of Europe to realize that their birth took place before aviation was a force. Such political fragmentation still hampers the freedom of aerial movement, for national frontiers are now three-dimensional and a nation's territories include the airspace above it. How much longer European air traffic will be hindered by national self-interest remains to be seen, but of the reality of the situation there is no doubt. The joint operation of the Scandinavian Airlines System by Norway, Sweden and Denmark seems a step in the right direction. So also is the preoccupation of such International bodies as I.C.A.O. and I.A.T.A. with the problems of the 'Freedoms of the Air'.

This, then, is the basis for any discussion of major world air routes. As a beginning it is useful to remember that the markets for air transport, as for its surface brethren, are fixed in certain well-defined regions of the world. Within these regions one finds the vast majority of large commercial airports. The spaces between are not so fixed and a degree of flexibility in the route chosen is possible, and it is here that the aircraft's advantages enable it to compete. Further, since the aeroplane is a new transport medium and will create its own field, it may simply supplement an existing pattern or originate a new one and pioneer new development.

Many attempts have been made to establish a 'centre of human gravity' on the Earth's surface and it is a well-known fact that the majority of human activity takes place within a hemisphere. As far back as 1899, A. Penck fixed the centre of a land hemisphere in which activity was concentrated, placing its centre south-west of Nantes. Raisz, and more recently Van Zandt,[2] have drawn attention to a similar orientation. A hemisphere centred on Nantes includes all the major land masses with the exception of Australia, the southern half of South America and Antarctica (*Fig. 1*).

Within this hemisphere are found not only the bulk of the world's cultivated land and mineral resources, but also 95% of its peoples, and 98% of industrial undertakings. At the centre lies Europe and the adjacent Mediterranean lands of North Africa and the Middle East, together accounting for 20% of the world population. Encircling Europe lie the two land masses of Asia and North America—home of the two greatest political powers of the present time. From such a disposition of the populated lands, Van Zandt distinguished a pattern of fundamental lines of movement (*Fig. 1*) connecting the various trade centres and serving as a first approximation of a world airway pattern. Note that these lines illustrated in *Fig. 1* do not represent actual airways; they simply serve as guides to present and future developments on a large scale. Two points are worthy of special mention and may be appreciated by a study of *Fig. 1*, i.e. (*a*) that the polar regions heralded as the 'crossroads' of the future are not in fact as important as some would suggest, (*b*) that Europe is nearer most other markets on the globe than any of its competitors—a result of its central position in the land hemisphere.

Whereas Van Zandt's observations provide a first approximation to the wherefore of world air routes, they only outline the manifest differences between the world's major regions. As a market for air transport, Asia is very different from Europe, to take one example. Europe includes a high proportion of industrialized communities with a high standard of living, while much of Asia still remains to be explored. Even where population density is high, as in China, the economy is based on an agricultural regime that provides little opportunity for the sort of trade favourable to a dense pattern of air routes.

The yardstick of a 'developed' country depends upon the purpose of the study and there are many possible indicators. For our purposes the economic development is the vital issue and, as suggested in the last chapter, the development of manufacturing industry is important. Provided we remember their limitations, the estimates made by the United Nations on the amount and distribution of national incomes are valuable here. In addition, the proportion of national income accruing from manufacturing activities is also significant. *Tables XVI–XVIII* give some sample figures, while *Fig. 7* embodies in map form the estimates for the seventy-two countries listed. The main air routes and the density of traffic using them are added for comparison. Fig. 7 takes account also of population distribution, since not the whole area of a country is important. For simplicity's sake, only those parts of a country where the population density exceeds five persons per square mile are shaded.

Perhaps the most startling fact to emerge from the tables is the dominating position of North America and particularly the United States. Europe likewise appears as a strongly developed area dominated by the countries of Western Europe, notably the United Kingdom, Sweden and Western Germany, France, the Low Countries and Switzerland. At the other extreme, the underdeveloped nature of the Asiatic countries stands out, particularly if one takes into account the density of population and potential resources.

Fig. 7 suggests the relationship of air traffic to the world's populated areas and together with *Table XIX* demonstrates the overwhelming importance of the developed countries in air transport.

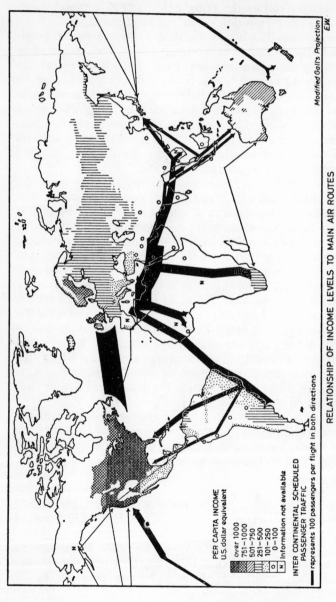

RELATIONSHIP OF INCOME LEVELS TO MAIN AIR ROUTES

Per capita income (United States dollar equivalent) plotted by states for areas with a population density of over five persons per square mile

Figure 7

TABLE XVI

NATIONAL INCOME 1962

Country	National Income (Million U.S. $)
Argentina	6,753
Australia	13,947
Belgium	10,297
Brazil	9,161
Canada	30,273
France	55,224
Western Germany	68,359
India	30,703
Netherlands	10,750
New Zealand	3,437
Pakistan	5,041
United Kingdom	63,410
United States	450,300
Yugoslavia	4,633
Switzerland	8,958
Sweden	11,338

Source: United Nations Yearbooks

TABLE XVII

PERCENTAGE OF NATIONAL INCOME
OBTAINED FROM MANUFACTURING INDUSTRY

Country	%
Canada	26·1
United States	29·2
Argentina	21·2
Pakistan	14·2
Japan	30·4
France	37·1
Western Germany	41·3
Belgium	31·3
United Kingdom	35·2

Note: Figures for other countries listed in previous table not available
Source: *United Nations Yearbook of National Accounts Statistics*

TABLE XVIII

RELATIVE POSITION OF THE CONTINENTS
IN TERMS OF POPULATION AND NATIONAL INCOME

	% Total World population 1962	% Total World income 1958*†	Per capita income all countries 1958 (U.S. equiv.)*†
Africa	8·6	3·2	115
Asia	56·3	11·2	107
USSR	7·0		
Europe	13·8	27·8	815
North America	8·8	51·2	1,780
Oceania	0·5	1·7	1,013
South America	4·8	4·9	322

* Based on Gross Domestic Product
† Excluding the communist states of Europe and Asia

Source: *United Nations Yearbook of National Accounts Statistics*

Before discussing the pattern of air routes as a whole, some further observations may be made from *Table XIX*. It will be noticed that not all the West European states enjoying a high *per capita* income originate high traffic densities. In particular, a comparison can be made between Switzerland and Sweden on the one hand, and the United Kingdom, the Netherlands and France on the other. Some further influence is responsible for this difference and it will be found that it is only those European states with strong overseas connections, or possessions, that are outstanding.

These tables suggest the basic reasons for the density of traffic on the major world airways. Of the international routes, the great North Atlantic bridge connecting the North American communities with Europe is by far the most outstanding feature (*Fig. 7*). Then follow European connections to Africa, the Middle and Far East and Oceania, and the routes between North and South America. We may now turn to consider the overall pattern, of which these airways form a dominant part, in more detail.

The map inside the front covers, showing the major world air routes, gives us the pattern. It should be remembered that this map does not show every single scheduled service, still less does it take account of the body of unscheduled routes. Air routes may

TABLE XIX

TOTAL REVENUE TRAFFIC ON SCHEDULED AIR SERVICES 1963

(Includes international and domestic operations of airlines registered in the Country)

Country	Passenger Kilometres Performed (Thousands)	Tonne-kilometres performed (Thousands) Freight and Excess Baggage	Mail
Argentina	880,689	8,687	3,423
Australia	3,892,109	94,168	28,459
Belgium	1,345,991	39,920*	4,357
Brazil	3,076,850	110,503	5,483
Canada	5,785,545	74,115	24,357
France	6,004,698	132,593*	38,089
India	1,689,393	53,507	15,175
Indonesia	328,193	5,303	1,211
Netherlands	2,564,247	128,043	13,366
New Zealand	626,276	12,679	1,628
Pakistan	710,236	28,597	3,257
Sweden	1,231,212	33,452	8,293
Switzerland	1,841,857	37,932*	9,601
United Kingdom	9,603,429	205,791	55,031
United States	71,437,828	1,661,946	537,016
West Germany	2,583,367	84,450	17,790
Yugoslavia	190,103	1,442	474

* Excess Baggage excluded.

Source: *I.C.A.O.*

be divided into two main groups—primary routes, which include the major international and domestic networks, and secondary routes, which may again be either international or domestic in character, but which serve to fill the interstices between the primary examples. The maps given show only the most important primary routes—international and domestic. We may define an international route simply as one that crosses the borders of more than one sovereign state, while a domestic route is internal to one particular state. Thus a trans-continental air route in the USA. must rank as a primary since it covers a great distance and serves widely different regions, even though it is 'domestic' in character. British domestic routes, on the other hand, are essentially secondary in comparison, with the possible exception of the London–Prestwick airway.

On the world map the internal network of the USA is the boldest feature of all, and is rivalled only by the shorter-range airways of Europe and the Mediterranean area. Taken together, these two nets, and the North Atlantic routes bridging them, form the densest air traffic zone on the Earth's surface. The airways of the USSR form a direct contrast to those of the USA and for a country of its size the cover is small. Around these major lines of movement has grown up an interconnecting maze of secondary routes and it is these that have shown enormous growth since 1945. Most interesting of this group are undoubtedly the pioneering lines in north Canada (*Fig. 11*), Australia and the less well-known northern routes of the USSR.

More minutely, it should be noted that direct transit between the major cities of the eastern seaboard of the USA and Canada with those of western Europe, is of recent origin, dating from 1957. Some traffic still takes the shortest sea crossing through Shannon, Eire, or Gander in Newfoundland. These two islands stand clear of the main land masses and represented useful staging points in the development of Atlantic routes. The presence of alternative routes both north and south of the Gander–Shannon track serves as a reminder that weather conditions play an important role in Atlantic routes. The northerly route followed chiefly in summer calls at Iceland and at either Gander or Goose Bay in Labrador. In the winter months the southerly route through the Azores may be used. Either alternative may be used at any period of the year according to weather conditions. Weather need not always be interpreted as a hazard, the route is chosen to take advantage of particular wind circulations and a longer traverse, that makes use of pressure and wind conditions to aid the passage, may prove the shortest in the end. With direct passage, the pattern has become more flexible, and traffic is no longer channelled through just a few cities like New York or London. Gander, Shannon, Iceland and the Azores still house radar aids and act as alternatives in case of technical trouble or bad weather. The present Gander–Shannon route lies as close to the great circle ideal as possible when all things are considered. Indeed, the North Atlantic routes provide a good example of the compromise that every air route must be.[1]

In contrast, the Pacific is comparatively empty. Initially, the presence of well-spaced island chains aided air routes to the Far East and Australia from the American continents, and they put in an appearance before the Atlantic examples. Traffic over the Pacific is minute compared with that over the Atlantic, and there are good reasons why this should be so. Trade between the Americas and Australasia is not so heavy as that between America and Europe, while the political situation reduces trade between America and the eastern countries of Asia. Even should trading prospects brighten in the latter case, there are good reasons why any increased air traffic should not take the trans-Pacific route. The map shows us that the shortest route from the western sea-board of North America to Japan and China is essentially an overland passage that passes northwards to Alaska, then along the outer Aleutian chain to northern China and Japan. Even from a point as far south as Batavia, the shortest route is similar. Until World War II such a route was a dream, for the lack of flying aids and the generally poor weather conditions made the route completely out of reach economically and technically. With the establishment of the air bridge from the USA through north-west Canada to Alaska and eastern Siberia during the war, the route was pioneered and flying aids and airfields established. Should the political situation favour increased American-Asiatic trade, this route bids fair to become an important highway. Indeed it represents one of the major 'airflows' suggested in *Fig. 1*. Even so, weather conditions must be reckoned with, and we may find alternative routes, using the island chains of the Pacific as alternative staging points, a regular feature—a situation made familiar in the Atlantic pattern.

European connections with the eastern countries of Asia and the southern continents of Africa and Australia reflect an earlier pattern of shipping lanes. Such routes were stimulated by the need for communications between Britain and the Commonwealth, France, Belgium and their possessions and the less-tangible relics of former colonial ties between European countries and overseas territories. The British case may serve as an example. Here the primary connections were between South Africa and Australia as the limiting points (omitting Atlantic routes). Between these two lay Britain's strategic foothold in the eastern Mediterranean, the Central and West African colonies and the far-eastern territories of India, Burma and Malaya. These countries were the keys to Britain's international air system—as they were for an earlier shipping pattern. Even with the independence of many former colonies in the post-war period, the economic and social ties

remain. In addition, the maintenance of strong air links between
these countries has a marked political flavour and the separation
of the purely economic from the picture is difficult if not impossible.

The plan of the air routes that arose from this situation differs
markedly from the usual notions of great circle ideals. Non-stop
transits to either South Africa or Australia and New Zealand are
not possible on technical grounds, and even if they were, such
transits would have to rely on sufficient traffic between Britain
and Australia alone to make them pay—an unlikely situation in
the foreseeable future. The South African route is a similar
example. The presence of intermediate points with strong ties
with Britain, and providing intermediate trade, has marked out
the stage lengths and directions to be taken. Should traffic
warrant a direct link with e.g. India or Australia, it is doubtful
if a direct great circle passage would prove the most economical.
In both cases the track would lie over the southern USSR and
the Himalayan ranges. The difficult physical conditions and the
associated lack of settlement, let alone flying aids, would make
the Himalayas a problem to be reckoned with, and the track
would still show a southerly 'bulge' in all probability. Nevertheless such a track represents one of the major features of *Fig. 1*,
but its use depends not a little on the possibility of intermediate
traffic in the USSR as well as in the countries further east.

British airline routes to Africa show a marked preference for
the eastern track linking Cairo and the Cape, with a smaller network skirting the western seaboard. One is tempted to suggest that
the Sahara has played an important role, but the bold lines crossing the desert between Libya and West Africa tend to indicate
that, as a purely physical barrier, the desert plays an increasingly
minor role. When French airways are added to the picture, the
impression is reinforced. British connections with the African
continent lie either in the eastern half of the continent or in the
coastal territories of West Africa, and this is the main reason for
the layout of the aerial pattern. No doubt the Sahara played its
part in determining which parts of the continent our colonial
forbears deemed worthy of attention, but to suggest that the
present air routes avoid the Sahara solely for purely physical
reasons is manifestly incorrect. Just as the Nile, the lakes and
rivers of eastern and southern Africa aided the explorer, so did
they favour the first air link with central and southern Africa.

Neither was the original choice of flying boats for this pre-1939 service as strange as might appear. The flying facilities set up for that pioneer route have played their part in establishing the present landplane services to South Africa. Any direct route from London (or Cairo for that matter) would lose the intermediate traffic to be found in central Africa.

West African routes were later arrivals, and here the Sahara played a more direct role. Between Europe and West Africa the Sahara lies astride direct communications and its lack of settlement discouraged air traffic, partly because there was no intermediate cargo to help airlines pay their way, and partly because a non-stop traverse was impossible technically. The earliest routes skirted the west coast, but West African connections failed to reach any stature until the post-war aeroplane made the trans-Sahara link an economic proposition. As distinct from local lines, major airways are now firmly established on the western side of the continent linking primarily with Britain, France and Belgium. One further point might be noticed. No direct link exists between North America and Africa. Traffic between these two continents is carried mainly by way of Europe. This apparently circuitous arrangement has sound economic foundations, for the amount of direct traffic does not warrant a highly developed connection. From the point of view of distance, too, the route through the western seaboard of Europe is shorter than any traverse through the Caribbean and Brazil.

Beyond the important gateway of the eastern Mediterranean, traffic is channelled eastwards to Pakistan and India. Most of this traffic originates in Western Europe, but important through-connections from North America are included. This route, skirting the mountain barriers of Baluchistan and the main mass of the Himalayas, is oriented towards Karachi, which has some foundation for its claim to be the 'gateway to the East'. From Karachi traffic either turns south for Colombo or eastwards for Calcutta. Of the two, the latter is the more important at present, for most routes to Indonesia and Australia follow the archipelago to Singapore, Djakarta and Darwin. Apart from the Cocos Islands, no good staging point exists between Colombo and the long ocean haul to Australia.

European traffic destined for the Far East is channelled through either Singapore or Bangkok, the former an important staging point since it also receives traffic from Australasia as we have seen. The political situation in China, and the lack of any market that results from it, necessitates a coastwise approach to Tokyo through Hong Kong. Further routes serve South Viet Nam by way of Bangkok and Saigon.

Connections between the two American continents are boldly apparent and show two distinct approaches. Most traffic leaves North America through Miami and connects through the stepping-stones of the West Indies to Port of Spain or Caracas, and thence south-eastwards to Belem, Rio de Janeiro and Buenos Aires. The loop round the eastern edge of the Amazon basin is a notable feature. The other approach takes a more westerly route from New Orleans or Houston through the states of Central America to Tocumen or Balboa in Panama. This route then passes south to Lima and Santiago, or from Lima across the waist of the continent to Rio and Buenos Aires. Taken together, these routes show the characteristic double loop round the southern part of the Gulf of Mexico and the Amazon basin.

Between the southern continents, in contrast, air routes are very thinly used. No route connects South America and Australia directly, while only the Qantas Empire Airways 'Springbok' service through the Cocos Isles and Mauritius connects Australia with Africa. Between South America and Africa the well-marked route from Recife to Dakar is essentially one stage on the Europe–South America airway. Very little traffic originates in Africa itself. Recife, on the eastern tip of Brazil and Dakar, on the western seaboard of Africa, are both important and busy airports that owe their position to the fact that the ocean crossing separating them is the shortest in the South Atlantic basin.

The importance of European connections with Latin-American states has already been alluded to and traffic to Brazil and Argentina is heavy. Many European operators serve one or more of these states. British participation has been rather sporadic under the aegis of BOAC, and its early predecessor, BSAA. Currently, the route is operated by British United Airways using VC–10 aircraft.

Such, then, is the pattern of world routes with one notable exception, the USSR. Little concrete material exists concerning the development of air transport in the Union, but we may note the bolder outlines of its pattern. In contrast to its continental neighbour, the United States, the USSR shows a much more open network, but one that appears to be filling in rapidly. The pattern of routes is strikingly like that of the United States in outline. In the latter, the densely populated and industrialized north-east has the densest pattern of airways in the continent and from it span the great trans-continental lines. In the USSR the nucleus lies between Moscow and Sverdlovsk with a marked radial pattern of routes serving European USSR as far south as Stalino, Rostov and Mineraljevodi. From this western concentration the trans-continental lines run east to Krasnoyarsk, Yakutsk, Khabarovsk and Vladivostok. The USSR does not appear to have a great tourist route comparable with the New York–Miami example in the USA. Of the airways of China, we know even less. CAAC (Civil Aviation Administration of China), centred on Peking, operates services eastwards and northwards to connect with Soviet carriers, and southwards to Chungking and Canton. A branch from Chungking serves the eastern cities of Hankow and Shanghai. The fact that the USSR and China between them control a large proportion of the land hemisphere is a reminder of the field that still lies open to the air transport operator.

We might ask ourselves finally what changes are likely to occur in the future pattern of world airways. A comparison of *Fig. 1* with the map of world air routes suggests that large-scale changes and additions would not be surprising, although the basic pattern is essentially complete. Much depends on the political situation and in particular on the relations between the western world and that of the USSR and China. It is here that great changes could occur. Among them we might find a strengthening of routes across the Arctic Circle between Asia and North America—e.g. from Northern Siberia (Magadan or Yakutsk) to Anchorage, Vancouver and Seattle—or westwards from Moscow through Greenland to the eastern seaboard of North America. The pattern of European routes could also be profoundly influenced by the relaxation of political tension. High-latitude great circle routes from London to Tokyo calling at Moscow and Peking represent a saving of about 1,300 miles over the currently employed route through India. To Australia through Moscow and southern Asia represents a smaller saving of distance (approximately 500 miles), but might well be worthwhile if intermediate traffic were available. Indeed it might be profitable to run services both north and south of the Himalayas to the Far East and Australia from Europe. The linking of the western European network with that of the USSR is a less conspicuous, but significant, possibility. From such a development the importance of such airports as Berlin and Warsaw would undoubtedly increase.

The polar route from western Europe through Greenland to Winnipeg and Los Angeles is a recent addition to Atlantic services. Such a route may never carry the traffic of the established North Atlantic passage, since so little intermediate traffic is available, but as a connection between Europe and western North America it has a strong pull. The logical extension of this route is the famous North-west passage from Europe to the Far East across North Greenland and Alaska to Tokyo, a route operated by Scandinavian Airlines from Copenhagen. It should be noted that these 'polar' routes do not in fact cross the geographical pole, indeed no foreseeable route does so. Whereas these high-latitude routes capture the imagination, it should be remembered that the lack of intermediate traffic in most cases suggests that the amount of traffic using them is likely to be limited.

Much speculation exists regarding the opening up of routes between the southern continents—so poorly developed at present. The Chilean government's intention to construct a major airport in the southern tip of Chile suggests that some foresee expansion. Nevertheless, the possibility of trans-Antarctican airways between South America and Australasia seems a much more remote possibility than the analogues of the Northern Hemisphere. Apart from the establishment of major routes, the 'filling in' of the basic pattern by secondary feeder services is a constantly expanding process. With the attention of the world turning to its undeveloped resources, the increase in such services is not surprising and we may expect further expansion in the future.

We may conclude with one further observation. The dominance of the United States and the growing strength of Soviet air transport are likely to result in these two great continental powers becoming the chief elements in the world picture. Whether any individual European country will be able to keep pace seems highly unlikely, for air transport on a grand scale is an expensive business. Taken together, European interests might continue to make an important and far-reaching contribution.

REFERENCES

1. Slater, John E. (See reference to Chapter 3.)
2. Van Zandt. (See references to Chapter 1.)
3. Davies, R. E. G. *A History of the World's Airlines.* 1964.

5

AIR TRANSPORT IN EUROPE

What is 'Europe'?

This may seem an odd question, but post-war economic and political changes have created many different associations of states. We must bear in mind, too, that the availability of statistics will depend a great deal on these groupings—e.g. 'Eastern' Europe, within the area of Soviet influence, publishes few figures that are comparable with those of Western Europe.

Geographically, Europe is well defined in the north, south and west by the sea, which forms an unmistakable frontier, even though the sea may be narrow in the south. To the east, a boundary is less easy to define. Europe is often spoken of as the 'western extension of Asia' for there is no physical break between Europe and Asia. The Ural Mountains are usually taken as a convenient dividing line, but they have never constituted a political frontier and are relatively easy to cross. From the Urals to the Caspian Sea stretches a 300-mile-wide plain, so often used by invading peoples from Asia. A more easily recognizable physical difference lies much further west, where the line from Kaliningrad, through the Pripet Marshes to the valley of the Bug and the Black Sea, divides the varied relief of the west from the lowlands of the western USSR. The area west of this line is still by no means an adequate unit, for the structural and topographical complexity of Scandinavia, Denmark, the Low Countries, France, Spain and the countries bordering the Mediterranean Sea is very different from the simpler landscapes of Eastern Germany and Poland. The latter more nearly belong to the zone of country east of the Pripet Marshes. This physical difference between eastern and western Europe has influenced the economic potential and the political development of the countries concerned. In turn, it has affected the trade and transport regimes and is, therefore, a division that is relevant.

Economically, Europe can be variously defined. Huntington's classification into Europe A—the industrial north-west and most advanced area economically, Europe C—the mainly agricultural countries of southern and south-eastern Europe, and Europe B —a transition zone between, is essentially a 'north–south' division of Europe. Again, one may differentiate the 'maritime' powers of the western seaboard from the 'continental' powers of eastern Europe. The former are characterized by their colonial developments and a large-scale participation in world trade. The British Isles, France, Belgium, the Netherlands, Spain and Portugal are the countries concerned, and indeed their economic history is notably different from Poland and the USSR. Germany shows characteristics of both kinds.

Since we are concerned with a medium of transport, trade regions are a valid standpoint. In his classic work *The Network of World Trade*, Folke Hilgerdt[4] distinguished Europe as far as European Russia as a distinctive trade region, but distinguished three divisions, i.e.:

(*a*) Continental Europe: industrial countries.
      (France, Belgium, Luxembourg, Netherlands, Sweden, Germany, Czechoslovakia, Switzerland, Austria and Italy.)
(*b*) Continental Europe: non-industrial countries.
      (Rest of Europe east of above countries.)
(*c*) Non-continental Europe.
      (United Kingdom, Ireland, Iceland.)

For the pre-war era upon which this division was made, the UK and the 'tropics' were the terminal points of a system of multilateral trade, with the USA and continental Europe in intermediate positions.

The upheavals of the 1930's, and more particularly World War II, upset this pattern. A study of United Nations' publications suggests that a system of division based on 'geography and currency' is now a more satisfactory basis, i.e.:

(*a*) The Sterling Area. (UK, Ireland, Iceland.)
(*b*) OEEC Europe.

(c) Eastern Europe. (Finland, Poland, Czechoslovakia, Hungary, Bulgaria, Rumania. Yugoslavia is 'marginal'.)

Such a classification shows similarities with Hilgerdt's division. Both are 'east–west', but the political influence of the 'Iron Curtain' is all too obvious in the later scheme. The separation of the UK from the continent is also worth noting.

The dominant political theme at the moment is the 'Iron Curtain' which effectively divides east from west. The United Nations' classification, already given, recognizes the division's importance from the economic point of view, particularly with reference to the compilation of statistics. Whereas this political fact may be only temporary in the long term, it is undoubtedly true to say that it has guided all post-war trade and development. Nevertheless, the present schism is more fundamental than might at first appear. Essentially, industrial Europe lies west of the line and agricultural Europe to the east. Such regional differences tend to foster trade and the main tragedy of the present political position is that normal inter-European trade has been disrupted. Berlin has felt the pull of both sides, for as the capital of pre-war Germany it had links with both the industrial west and the predominantly agricultural eastern zones of the country. The almost complete lack of surface contact with Western Germany since 1945 has fostered the air link between Berlin and the west. Air transport manifestly operates under a 'forced draught'.

Hilgerdt's division of continental Europe recognized the significance of trade between east and west, and it is no accident that his division so closely resembles the present position. The United Kingdom has always tended to stand apart from the political affairs of the continent, except where the balance of power was concerned. Up to 1939 her interests were more firmly fixed in the Commonwealth and Empire than in Europe. Since 1945 some reorientation has been discernible, but it has not occurred at the expense of former ties. The attitude to the Coal and Steel Community, both in the early stages of that body's formation and since, has shown this fact.

The complexity of Europe has been sufficiently demonstrated, and within the boundary of the traditional geographical definition we might consider air transport under widely differing conditions. Such a study, commendable as it might be, must be foregone, since we do not possess enough information concerning post-war transport in Eastern Europe. Here, we shall consider only Western

Europe, including within that definition countries west of a line through, but including, Sweden, Western Germany, Austria and Italy. The United Kingdom will be considered as part of this region.

Within this area are included all the 'economically developed' European countries as defined in an earlier chapter and it is with these that we are most particularly concerned, since they provide the bulk of the traffic. Where reference is made to a wider concept, the term 'Greater Europe' will be used. In this case the eastern boundary will be taken to include countries as far east as Finland, Poland, Czechoslovakia and Rumania.

Western Europe : World position and physical setting

The position of Western Europe in a global sense is of fundamental importance. *Fig. 1* shows that Europe is situated between the two great land masses of the Northern Hemisphere. Many routes between the two continents of North America and Asia pass over or near Europe, which forms, therefore, a marked nodal area. Flanking Europe to the south lie the continents of Africa and South America—two of the major land masses of the Southern Hemisphere. As Van Zandt noted, the average flight distance from Europe to each of the other principal trading regions of the Earth is less than for any other trading area. For a vehicle that ignores differences of land and sea, this fact is of fundamental importance. No longer need mountain chains or sea ice force all transport connections to show a strong east–west component. *Table XX* gives some great circle distances that permit comparison between various cities.

Since Europe's position is so central, one might expect traffic to converge upon the continent from all the primary directions. Apart from the fact that air routes are channelled into definite airways served by radio aids, air traffic does not in fact approach from all directions. Two major 'gateways' only affect Western Europe, and a third only reaches Eastern Europe. Traffic from the direction of the Arctic Circle is at present very thin, but may increase in the future. In Western Europe, by far the heaviest traffic comes from North America (*see* map on pages 8–9) and reaches Europe through the great airports of London and Paris. The other major channel serves Africa, South America, the Far East and Oceania and converges on the Mediterranean airports. In Western Europe, Rome and Marseilles are notable, but they

TABLE XX

GREAT CIRCLE DISTANCES
(*Statute miles*)

	London	New York	Moscow	Cape Town	Tokyo
New York	3,475				
Moscow	1,550	4,665			
Cape Town	6,010	8,940	6,300		
Tokyo	5,940	6,740	4,650	9,155	
Sydney	10,555	10,200	9,005	6,840	4,860

form part of a wider group of airports that includes Athens Cairo and Beirut. As far as Western Europe is concerned, the eastern gateway to Asia is relatively unimportant, for most traffic stops at Berlin. Should trade increase between east and west, then we may expect Berlin and Warsaw, together with Stockholm and Budapest in the north and south respectively, to take on the stature of major European airports.

Within Greater Europe itself, the outstanding fact in air transport is the short distances between the major cities. *Table XXI* gives some sample airline distances and it will be seen that the majority fall within the 'short stage' category—i.e. from

200–500 miles. When compared with the USA, European air transport is a short-range system—with all that that means.

Although the smallest continent (under any definition), Europe contains a higher proportion of cultivable land than any other, and good mineral wealth, especially coal. The structural trend of Europe favours varied relief and gives rise, among other things, to an indented coastline of great length. Such a characteristic means that most lowland areas have ready access

TABLE XXI

AIRLINE DISTANCES BETWEEN EUROPEAN CITIES
(Airport–airport distance. Statute miles)

London–Paris	226	Amsterdam–Glasgow	440
„ –Brussels	215	„ –Rome	810
„ –Amsterdam	231	„ –Copenhagen	392
„ –Glasgow	326	„ –Oslo	569
„ –Rome	906		
„ –Copenhagen	607	Paris–Brussels	122
„ –Oslo	715	„ –Amsterdam	252
„ –Madrid	881	„ –Rome	688
„ –Lisbon	1,058	„ –Copenhagen	628
		„ –Madrid	640
Rome–Athens	648	„ –Lisbon	905

to the sea and to each other. The importance of such 'inland' seas as the Baltic or the Mediterranean on the growth of European states is far-reaching, for flanking them are the lowlands of the North European Plain, the Paris and London basins, Aquitaine and the smaller lowlands of the Mediterranean. Water transport —especially coastal traffic—is an essential element in European transport.

On land, Europe is again fortunate. With the exception of the mountains of Alpine age, no great mountain barriers disrupt surface movement and even the Alps, the highest ranges, are passable at many points. Deserts are completely absent. Much of Europe, therefore, is eminently accessible by land. Dominating the landscape in the north, the North European Plain stretches from European Russia and Eastern Europe to the outliers of the Paris Basin and the lowlands of S.E. England. The basin of Aquitaine and the Rhône lowlands provide access to the western Atlantic shores and the Mediterranean, while southwards across the Alpine passes, or along the line of the Danube, access to the northern plain of Italy and the Hungarian plain further east is available. Surface transport, then, has fewer physical obstacles to its development than on any other continent—a useful corollary to the fact that distances are short.

There are contrasts, however. Western Europe with its varied landscape of mountain, valley, hill and plain, built up on complex structural vertebrae, contrasts with the physical monotony of Eastern Europe—an area of structural stability and spacious plains. Complications occur only in the Urals and in the folded regions of the south. No sharp break between east and west exists, but rather a zone of transition, while some features show little apparent difference in east or west Europe. Finally, along the foreland zone of the Hercynian structures, occur the coalfields of the continent, stretching from South Wales to France, Belgium and Germany, thence across Silesia to the Donets basin.

Since physical barriers of any size are so unimportant, one must look for more subtle surface differences in order to descry an advantage for the air transport world. By far the most significant 'barriers' to surface movement are the seas. In particular, the English Channel is outstanding, for despite its narrow extent, transhipment is still necessary when travelling from the UK to the continent. The Baltic and Mediterranean are likewise important from this viewpoint. The Alpine mountains bestow a small advantage to air transport, but, thanks to well-defined passes, the advantage is a limited one physically. It is probably more accurate to say that the Alps influence surface transport, but do not prevent it. Air routes, therefore, that cross seas or the mountains are more likely to grow in importance than those connecting points involving no surface transhipment. That some of the former are also over longer distances is an added advantage.

Climatically, Europe again poses no great problems to surface transport. Problems of heavy snowfall are rarely important to rail or road, no marked rainy season brings floods to undermine or destroy roads and tracks, and on the other hand no prolonged drought makes water supply a critical factor. Fog, perhaps, is important in North-west Europe, but fog affects air transport far more than road or rail in any case. Indeed, the quickly changing variety of European weather affects air transport more than any other medium. In particular, fog, 'smog', and low visibility associated with frontal systems, are the chief hazards to Europe's crowded airways and airports. Icing, too, is an important element at all seasons, but particularly in winter. The fact that no prolonged adverse periods of weather usually occur does not detract from the fact that aircraft must still sacrifice weight and performance to the necessity of providing means of combating ice and poor visibility. At airports—the critical points—extensive radio aids are essential for high-density operations throughout the year. Since most airports are on lowland sites near great cities, smog is always a hazard, while the lowland itself may act as a track for depressions.

One further aspect of climate needs to be noticed. Since air transport derives most of its revenue from passenger traffic, tourism is important. About half its revenue may be derived from tourist traffic at certain seasons. Climate plays a big part here, in association with relief. The attractive climate of the Mediterranean countries, often allied with mountain scenery, have helped to create the great tourist centres of these areas. Winter sports in the Alpine resorts account for a flow of winter season traffic. Scandinavia likewise benefits from climatic conditions, both in summer and winter. When to these facts are added the cultural attractions of Europe—which attract overseas tourists—it can be seen that both overseas and inter-European tourism is a very important element in European air transport.

Population and resources: market potential

Since air transport derives so much of its revenue from passenger traffic, the distribution of population is an important consideration. In addition, economic development must be advanced to supply the business and tourist potential. The general position in Europe may be judged from *Tables XVI, XVII* and *XVIII*, but some slight expansion is needed here.

In terms of population numbers, Greater Europe represents one of the greatest concentrations of mankind on the Earth. Within Western Europe some 300 millions are accounted for. Perhaps of greater significance is the fact that the 'Soviet bloc'—which includes the USSR—has a population of 1,000 millions (one third of mankind); as far as Western Europe is concerned, this is largely an untapped market. *Table XXII* presents the picture in more detail.

The areas of greatest population density lie in the predominantly industrialized zones of the UK, Belgium and Western Germany, with the central lowlands of Scotland as an outlier.

To this belt of dense population must be added the hardly less significant concentrations of central and northern France, the Netherlands, Denmark and the north Italian Plain. The latter groups depend either on a specialized agriculture as in Denmark, or upon a more 'mixed' economy like France and Northern Italy. Areas of low population density are mainly those where physical conditions, including resources, are poor. Except for the coastal lowlands, Scandinavia and Spain illustrate the position, while the mountainous territories of parts of Switzerland, Austria, Greece and Italy show low densities also. Of great importance is the concentration of peoples in the major cities, particularly the capitals and large industrial towns. Greater London (8·5 million) and Greater Paris (6 million) are outstanding, but cities like Glasgow, Birmingham, Milan and Hamburg are scarcely less important from this viewpoint. It is to the great industrial countries and their packed cities that air transport looks for most of its traffic potential. The cities are likely to rank as the nodal points of the European air network.

A dense population is only a part of the story and on its own does not necessarily give rise to traffic. Air-passenger traffic may be broadly categorized as business or tourist by nature, although the dividing line may be thin and there are, of course, other reasons for air travel that do not quite fit either category—e.g. differences between those travelling on company as opposed to private business, or those travelling to visit relatives—i.e. 'for family reasons'.[3] Business traffic depends on the development of industry and commerce and on the degree of trade existing between one area and another. *Table XXIII* shows the scale of foreign trade of European countries.

When it is remembered that the first five nations of the world (i.e. USA, Canada, UK, Western Germany, France) account for 48% of the world's exports and 43% of imports, the importance of the industrial countries of Western Europe will be appreciated. Such trade is likely to foster business travel for the airlines both within Europe and overseas. *Table XXIV* illustrates the importance of inter-European trade—the aspect we are most concerned with. The same table shows, too, the importance of extra-European trade to the UK particularly.

Enough has now been said to illustrate the market potential in size and distribution for business traffic. We should remember that not only passenger traffic, but freight carriage also,

TABLE XXII

POPULATION: EUROPE AND USSR 1961

State	Population (millions)	Area (Thous. sq. miles)
WESTERN EUROPE:		
United Kingdom	52·7	63·2
Ireland	2·8	18·2
Iceland	0·2*	26·7
France (1962)	46·5	142·7
Luxembourg	0·3	0·7
Belgium	9·2	7·9
Netherlands	11·6*	8·7
Denmark	4·6	11·1
Sweden	7·5	116·3
Norway	3·6	84·0
Western Germany	53·9	—
Switzerland	5·4	10·7
Austria	7·1	21·7
Portugal	8·9	23·8
Spain	30·5	130·3
Italy	49·9	78·0
Greece	8·4	34·3
Total	303·1	778·3
EASTERN EUROPE		
Finland	4·5	87·3
Eastern Germany	17·1*	—
Poland	29·7	80·7
Czechoslovakia	13·7	33·1
Hungary	10·0	24·9
Yugoslavia	18·5	66·5
Rumania	18·5*	61·5
Bulgaria	7·9*	28·7
Albania	1·6	7·4
Total	121·5	390·1
USSR	216·2	8,400·0

(Soviet Bloc—USSR, China, Mongolia, North
Vietnam, Eastern Europe = 1,015 million
population)

* Estimated

Sources: *United Nations Demographic Yearbook*
Statesman's Year Book

TABLE XXIII

VALUE OF FOREIGN TRADE—EUROPE

(US $ millions)
1962

State	Value	
	Exports	*Imports*
Western Germany	13,273	12,392
United Kingdom	11,059	12,578
France	7,365	7,521
Italy	4,675	6,085
Netherlands	4,584	5,347
Belgium-Luxembourg	4,325	4,556
Sweden	2,922	3,114
Switzerland	2,230	3,021
Denmark	1,658	2,128
Austria	1,263	1,551
Norway	972	1,654
Finland	1,104	1,228
Spain	734	1,569
Ireland	487	765

Remaining countries less than 1,000 million $ total trade
Source: International Monetary Fund, *Direction of Trade*

will be affected by this pattern. Travel for business reasons is not always the important source of passenger revenue that is sometimes imagined. On many routes, tourists are far more in evidence. The ability to take advantage of air travel for holiday purposes depends a great deal on income level and social conditions. Whereas a high *per capita* income is likely to favour tourist travel in any given country, habits and social distinctions may also play a part. *Table XVI* showed the level of national income and one may perceive from that table that western countries appear to hold the highest market potential in Europe as a whole. By far the greatest part of this potential is directed towards European resorts, mainly as the result of the actual income levels, but also because of currency restrictions, e.g. North America is a 'hard' currency area for many countries and dollars are not available for tourists. One should not assume, however, that it is only those in the higher income groups that travel by air. Party travel—often by charter service—is important, especially where air companies

TABLE XXIV

DIRECTION OF TRADE—EUROPE

Exports by value (US $ millions) for leading European countries
in 1962

	N. America	Latin America	Common Market	Other West Europe	E. Europe and USSR	Middle East	Rest of Asia	Rest of Africa	Oceania
				Destination					
UK	1525	457	2188	2295	369	550	1215	1237	966
West Germany	1103	788	4514	4060	505	395	771	428	149
France	478	283	2713	1198	267	153	252	1498	66
Belgium-Luxembourg	457	131	2459	542	87	92	115	168	23
Netherlands	232	139	2256	727	76	112	210	206	33
Sweden	186	126	962	831	154	47	72	81	44

Source: International Monetary Fund. *Direction of Trade*

use low-rate party tickets. Fitzgerald[3] has pointed out that income
level may not be the only, or even the best, criterion of tourist
potential. Occupation status helps to determine not only business
travel, but tourist also. Thus, as Fitzgerald suggested, a young
professional man with family responsibilities might be unable to
afford a holiday by air, even though his salary exceeded £1,000
per annum. On the other hand a skilled industrial worker with
family, earning £12 a week (£624 p.a.), frequently puts aside funds
for a holiday from his surplus earnings. The latter worker may
be a far better target for sales promotion than his professional
colleague. In brief, therefore, while recognizing income level as
a yardstick, we should remember that it may not be the best one.

The source of tourist potential is less easy to define, therefore.
Not only will the peoples of industrial Europe provide a source,

but a much wider, if less concentrated, potential will exist in other countries. The centres of tourist attraction are a simpler aspect of the problem. Here, it is difficult to distinguish inter-European from overseas traffic statistically, although qualitatively the position is clearer. Broadly, three main tourist centres may be discerned in Europe:

(a) Scandinavia.
(b) United Kingdom.
(c) France-Switzerland-Austria-Italy. ('Alpine' and 'Mediterranean' resorts.)

Of these, the last (c) is by far the most important with a total influx of over eight million tourists a year (using all forms of transport). Italy, with a high proportion of French and Swiss tourists, heads the list, but most of these use rail travel over the short distances involved. France, with tourists from Belgium, Switzerland, UK and USA predominating, is a more important centre from the point of view of the airlines. The UK attracts fewer continental visitors than she sends out, but, when American and Commonwealth visitors are added, must rank as an important centre. Scandinavian tourist flows show a high proportion of inter-Scandinavian traffic—especially of Danes to Swedish resorts and cities—but the UK, France and the USA also contribute a proportion, many of whom fly in order to avoid surface transhipment.

The importance of climatic conditions on the popularity of (c) has already been alluded to. For many European tourists, this probably weighs heavily. Overseas visitors are more likely to find family connections and the attraction of Europe as a cultural centre more compelling. Indeed, Europe's standing as an international tourist centre rests mainly on the fact that it is regarded as the home of western civilization.

So far we have been discussing passenger traffic chiefly from the point of view of the scheduled airline. We must take note, finally, of the fact that a proportion of passenger traffic—albeit a small one—uses charter services. Apart from business and tourist motives, a much wider field is open here. Party travel has been mentioned as an aspect of tourism, but urgent necessity provides a source for the chartered aircraft, e.g. the carriage of medical staff and patients. The movement of pilgrims, scouts,

Olympic teams and theatrical companies all involve sufficient numbers to warrant aircraft charter. Shipping companies often ferry relief crews by air in order to keep their ships available for longer periods of service, without the necessity of returning to the home port to change crews. Such movements provide work for the charter company.

Freight traffic, by comparison with passenger traffic, is at present small. Unfortunately, too, statistics of freight movements in Europe are scattered and incomplete. Freight can be carried either by scheduled passenger services, by scheduled cargo service, or by charter agreement. Since freight is shipped by relatively few people and is usually flown only one way, there is a considerable field for the charter company. Potential sources of traffic are more diffuse, but the industrial areas again prove important, and over-water routes are outstanding. Specialized services like the cross-channel car ferry of British United Air Ferries are an example of highly successful services that must be looked upon mainly as 'freight' operations. *Table XXV* shows the phenomenal growth of this service, which would have been impossible, be it noted, without the specialized freighter aircraft. Such a service fills a need that can only be provided by surface transport at the expense of transhipment time and costs. The type of cargo carried by air can be seen from *Table XII* and the importance of manufactured commodities stands out. The direction of traffic flow cannot be so readily shown, since statistics are not available. Some examples will be given at a later stage.

The pattern of air traffic

The most striking features of the air-route pattern are the large number of routes involved and the disparity in their relative importance. The concentration of activity in north-west Europe is marked, for here a dense network connects the larger cities, many of which are very closely spaced. No stage in this zone exceeds 500 miles and many lie between 200 and 350 miles—in fact a helicopter protagonist's dream! Close scrutiny of *Fig. 8* shows that all the routes of whatever importance are short, and the feature is not confined only to the denser areas. More particularly, the over-water and trans-Alpine routes show up much as one would expect them to. In Scandinavia, the difficult terrain and scattered resources have created an important internal network, and in addition, Scandinavian international routes provide a source of income out of proportion to the internal potential.

TABLE XXV

BRITISH UNITED AIRWAYS CROSS-CHANNEL SERVICES
(Inaugurated July 1948)

Year	Total number of vehicles transported
1948	170
1949	2,700
1950	3,850
1952	10,900
1954	43,000
1957	45,500
1960	115,000
1962	137,500
1963	128,550

Sources: *Silver City Airways Air Ferry Guide British United Air Ferries*
Figures from 1957 include 'Channel Air Bridge'. In 1964 Silver City became part of British United Air Ferries

This is a modern example of an old characteristic—the carrying trade of Scandinavian shipping.

The impression of density in the European network is not without foundation, for it has been estimated[6] that there are twice as many routes in Europe as there are in the USA. This is an almost direct reversal of the proportions of European–USA mileages in rail and road transport. We should remember that air mileage includes not only the characteristic 'direct link' between cities, but also the mileage of stopping routes between the same cities. *Table XXVI* shows the comparative mileages in Europe and the USA. The reasons for this apparently abnormal air mileage are not far to seek. Europe represents a conglomeration of sovereign states, between which little regulation of air routes has existed. Each country has set up its air routes—many with Government support—mainly through the medium of bilateral agreements with the countries they wished to serve. In

TABLE XXVI

ROUTE MILEAGES: WESTERN EUROPE* AND USA 1953

	Europe	USA
Population (millions)	320	160
Area (million square miles)	1,350	3,020
Road mileage	1,109,000	2,118,000
Railway mileage	126,000	227,000
Air route mileage	186,000	93,200

Source: Wheatcroft[6]

* Western Europe includes here Finland, Greece and Turkey

contrast, the USA represents a single political unit, within which the regulating function of the Civil Aeronautics Board has restricted the indiscriminate extension of air routes. If all the 200 applications or more made to the CAB for air routes each year were granted, the position would be very different.

The air network may now be treated in more detail and we may consider, first, the routes themselves and then the relation of routes to the cities served. Finally, we may return to consider the network as a whole and in terms of individual airline routes.

Although statistics relating to the origin and destination of passengers are difficult to obtain in detail, such studies as have been possible reveal an enormous variation in the traffic flow on European routes. Thus out of almost 200 routes, some 42 major ones, with capacities of more than 100 passengers/day, account for 61% of the total daily seat/miles. Nearly all these routes lie in the developed countries of Western Europe (*Fig. 8* and *Table XXVII*) and are operated by European airlines. '5th Freedom'* traffic is not included in the total. Routes that cross water account for 70% of the total,[6] if one includes the France–North Africa routes. The significance of the English Channel is very marked, and we shall return to this feature again when we come to study the cities involved on Channel routes. Again, the density of traffic between Copenhagen and Stockholm owes much to the fact that they are separated by the Sound at the entrance to the Baltic. Much of this traffic is undertaken by the aircraft of the Scandinavian Airlines System (SAS)—a joint organization owned by Denmark, Norway and Sweden. This may also help to account

* *See* Appendix.

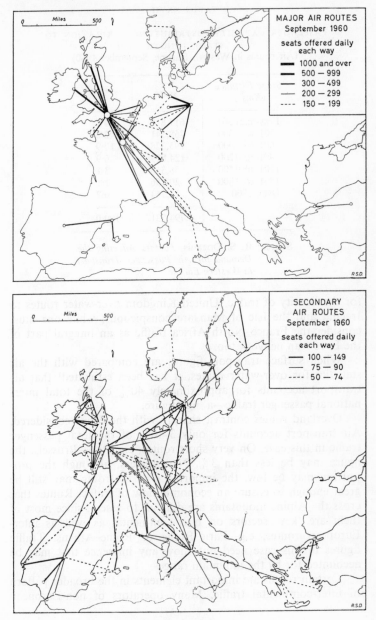

Figure 8 Air traffic in Europe

TABLE XXVII

PASSENGER CAPACITY DISTRIBUTION IN RELATION TO
STAGE LENGTH
(Air routes in Western Europe, September 1960)

Stage Distance (Kms.)	Seats	%
Less than 301	617,818	34·5
301 to 600	768,341	42·8
601 to 900	195,328	10·9
901 to 1200	124,829	6·9
1201 to 1500	56,516	3·1
1501 to 1800	20,156	1·1
Over 1800	11,743	0·7
	1,794,731	100·0

Source: R. S. Doganis, *Factors Affecting the Demand for Air Passenger Transport in Western Europe*

for the density of traffic. United Kingdom over-water routes to Ireland and the Isle of Man are conspicuous, while one must consider the France–North Africa traffic as an integral part of the European network too.

When surface transport figures are compared with the air statistics for over-water routes, it has been estimated[1] that air transport accounts for approximately 40% of the total international passenger traffic—a high figure.

Overland routes contrast sharply with these just considered. Air transport accounts for only 3–10% of the total passenger traffic in this case. On very short routes, e.g. Paris–Brussels, the figure may be less than 3%. Nevertheless, although the proportion may be low, the importance of the route may still be great enough to ensure an economic flow of traffic. Routes that cross the Alpine mountains are difficult to assess, since most of them are 'key' sectors on inter-continental as well as inter-European routes, e.g. Paris–Rome or Rome–Athens. Traffic figures in this case need not show any influence that may be accounted for by the mountain ranges.

Certain routes are important elements in the broader pattern of inter-continental traffic. Many operators of non-European origin operate over these routes and 5th Freedom traffic must be assessed. Except for certain key sectors of this kind, 5th Freedom traffic probably accounts for only about 2–3% of the total inter-European traffic. Routes in Germany must be considered an exception. Key sectors on the inter-continental routes are:

> Rome–Athens
> Athens–Istanbul
> London–Glasgow (Prestwick)
> London–Shannon
> Paris–Rome

On the Rome–Athens sector, for example, some 10 airlines have services. Of the ICAO members, 20 serve London. It will be noted that the airports and sectors concerned are the western and southern 'gateways' to Europe already suggested.

Routes in Germany are a special case, since they were operated by the occupying powers. The reinstatement of German-operated airlines is now established and in the future we may expect a more normal route network. The importance of German routes up to date has stemmed from the political situation. Much traffic was undoubtedly concerned with the movement of officials and servicemen. *Table XXVIII* shows the extent of the traffic under these conditions in 1953. The importance of the US airline, Pan American World Airways, resulted from the status of the USA as an occupying power at that time, and in a sense PAA was a 'European' airline. PAA's German services accounted for 5% of the total non-European participation of 8% in European routes. *Table XXVIII* illustrates the importance of the German services to European airlines like BEA and Air France. The return of German-operated airlines has decreased the importance of German routes to these airlines.

Berlin, isolated by the Russian zone from Western Germany, relied up to 1954–55 almost entirely on an air link. Since that period, surface transport has become easier and the importance of the Berlin air services has decreased to something more approaching a 'normal' level. The 'normal' role of Berlin in any free system of air routes—i.e. with the opening up of opportunities for Western European operators in Eastern Europe and the USSR—would still be an important one, for the city is sited in the path of any future routes to those areas. It is, like London,

TABLE XXVIII

INTERNAL GERMAN TRAFFIC, SUMMER 1953

Airline	Percentage of total seat miles	German traffic as percentage of total European traffic of airlines concerned
PAA (USA)	39·0	85·3
BEA	28·0	12·5
Air France	17·0	19·1
SAS	8·5	5·8
Sabena	3·0	5·0
KLM	2·5	3·0
Swissair	2·0	3·0
Total	100·0	11·5

Source: Air Research Bureau[1]

Rome or Athens, a gateway to countries outside Europe. The future may see the sector Berlin–Warsaw becoming as cosmopolitan as the Rome–Athens sector.

A close study of *Fig. 8* reveals that a large proportion of routes are direct city–city connections. Many of these rank as minor routes and carry a small proportion of traffic. The minor routes in any area might well be taken as 'feeders' to the more important international routes. That Europe's examples do not seem to fill this requirement is suggested by the maps. So short are the sectors between the cities on the major routes that the minor services appear too dense to serve purely in the capacity of feeder lines.

Distance is an important element, and the key to the European network lies in the fact that it is a short-stage network. On many of the major routes involving short-stage lengths a water crossing is involved, but on others—e.g. Brussels–Paris (156 miles) or Amsterdam–Brussels (104 miles)—this is not so, and the stage distance, moreover, is well below the 'economic minimum' suggested for fixed-wing aircraft in an earlier chapter. Such anomalies may seem to indicate a highly uneconomic regime in this pre-helicopter era. That such routes deserve the title 'major', and do prove economic in practice, is a phenomenon we must consider later. More predictable, perhaps, are the low load factors found on some of the short minor routes—many averaging only 40%. This again suggests that the minor routes are too dense.

The seasonal nature of the traffic flow is also an essential feature, particularly as passengers are the chief source of revenue.

The graph (*Fig. 9*) illustrates the nature of the seasonal flow in the case of BEA and shows the movements that have characterized recent years. Seasonal fluctuations are, of course, a far more serious phenomenon to the operator of short-stage routes than to his long-range colleagues, since, in order to maximize revenue, a high intensity of operations with the maximum possible traffic flow is needed. Seasonal fluctuations, by operating against this requirement, pose severe problems. In some ways the operator appears to be in a cleft stick, since in order to increase revenue and reduce operating costs he needs large-capacity aircraft, but these are not justified without the traffic to sustain them. That BEA have been able to make progress in stabilizing their annual flow is a noteworthy achievement. It must be remembered, too, that operational staff requirements are largely controlled by peak periods of operation, so that the larger the seasonal variation, the lower the productivity of the staff is likely to be.

Fig. 9 illustrates another aspect of seasonal differences that is important. The main seasonal variation occurs in passenger traffic, whereas mail and freight show much lower oscillations. A characteristic of aircraft at the present time is their relative lack of specialization, most aircraft carrying passengers, mail and freight. Thus, unless the seasonal variations are the same for all classes of traffic, unused capacity will occur. In brief, to meet the passenger peak in summer, aircraft will have to 'carry' unwanted freight and mail space.

Table XXIX shows the difference tourist class traffic brings in the capacity of certain present airliners. Such developments are not possible without the traffic density to support them.

One further feature of the seasonal pattern needs to be noted. Within the broader swings there occur smaller traffic differences. Thus passenger traffic—especially tourist—shows a peak at week-ends, while freight becomes available during the week, since most firms close down at the week-ends. This again would seem to pose difficulties for the 'mixed-traffic' aircraft and provide scope for specialization in aircraft type. Again, traffic density is the

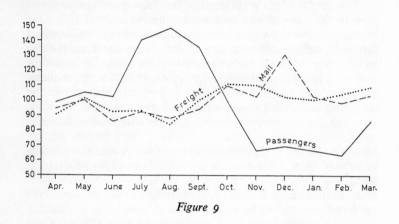

Seasonal Variations of Traffic Types
British European Airways
1963-64
Average month=100

Figure 9

TABLE XXIX

PASSENGER CAPACITY OF AIRCRAFT

Aircraft	Mixed 1st and Tourist Class seating capacity	Maximum Tourist 'high density' seating capacity
At present used on European routes:		
Caravelle	75	94
Comet IV B	89	102
Trident	82	103
Larger aircraft used mainly on long-stage operations.		
Boeing 707–320	120	189
DC–8	127	189
VC–10	115	151

Source: *Flight International*

key, for without a sufficiently high potential the specialization becomes uneconomic. Such seasonal differences are characteristic of the European network. That they apply to all countries is perfectly true, but few have to contend with the short-stage routes that European operators are faced with. We might note, finally, that August is the peak month for passenger traffic— even the aeroplane seems tied to school holidays!

We may now look at the European network from a somewhat different, yet inter-related, standpoint. From the previous discussion it would appear that the density of traffic on any route depends on the size of the settlements served and the distance between them. Traffic flow tends to vary directly with population and inversely with the stage length. The question is, how far does size of settlement affect flow? Is the relationship in fact so simple?

We may begin by comparing the density of traffic on any route with the population of the cities served by that route. From *Fig. 8* it will be seen that the bulk of the European traffic is accounted for by the routes connecting the great cities of the manufacturing belt of Western Europe. The axis of this system is the London to Paris route, with these two cities as the important settlements. Closely surrounding them lie other densely populated towns. How far do London and Paris 'blanket' these centres— i.e. produce a 'traffic shadow'? Do all large cities produce traffic proportional to their size?

Table XXX attempts to bring together all the revelant information. Unfortunately, no reliable figures for the origin and destination of passengers for Europe as a whole exist. Limited returns by country of origin and destination were made available by ICAO up to 1952, but have now ceased. This is a distinct disadvantage, particularly as adequate returns are available for the United States. No completely comparable analysis may be made of the networks in the two continents. *Table XXX* attempts an approximate estimate of the required relationship between traffic generated by a city and its population, by two substitute methods.

Column (*b*) *Table XXX* plots the cities served by airlines using the city named in the first column. Account is taken of both domestic and international traffic, and includes both direct transits and those requiring one or more stop-overs. On the face of it, the more important the city, the more likely it is to have good

TABLE XXX

SERVICE AND CAPACITY INDICES. EUROPE

Population greater than 1 million	Population (nearest 100,000) (a)	Cities served by airlines 1953–54 (b)	Seats per day 1953 (c)	Service Index (d)	Capacity index (e)	Functions (f)
London	40	247	3,913	138	284	Capital. Port
Manchester	10	72	345	160	100	Industrial
Birmingham	10	48	100	100	29	Industrial
Glasgow	10	103	267	229	78	Industrial. Port
Berlin	30	32	1,360	20	132	Occupied by Allies
Hamburg	20	62	706	69	102	Industrial. Port
Rome	20	104	616	115	89	Capital
Milan	10	41	265	91	77	Industrial
Naples	10	11	50	24	15	Tourist
Madrid	20	69	375	77	54	Capital
Barcelona	10	37	385	82	112	Regional centre. Tourist
Paris	30	121	2,188	90	211	Capital
Vienna	20	31	192	34	28	Capital
Athens-Piraeus	10	78	310	189	90	Capital
Population less than 1 million						
Amsterdam	8	110	1,597	310	576	Port. Industrial
Antwerp	3	5	50	36	39	Port
Basle	2	24	80	267	116	River port. Tourist
Berne	1	1	10	20	30	Capital
Bordeaux	3	21	100	150	97	Port
Bremen	4	15	120	83	87	Port
Bristol	4	8	10	45	7	Port
Brussels	9	106	1,134	236	327	Capital
Cologne	6	6	95	22	46	River Port. Industrial
Copenhagen	9	93	1,638	227	474	Capital
Dublin	5	62	700	270	405	Capital
Düsseldorf	5	65	587	295	339	River Port. Industrial
Edinburgh	4	34	25	189	18	Regional centre. Tourist
Frankfurt	5	87	1,179	400	680	Industrial
Geneva	1	66	531	733	1,520	International centre
Göteborg	3	38	430	271	414	Port
Hanover	4	10	530	56	384	Regional centre
Lisbon	7	62	94	194	39	Capital
Lyons	5	9	16*	41	9*	Industrial
Munich	8	26	393	72	142	Regional centre
Newcastle	3	13	25	100	24	Industrial. Port
Nice	2	58	435	644	631	Tourist
Nuremberg	4	11	120	61	87	Industrial. Tourist
Oslo	4	67	328	373	237	Capital
Reykjavik	0·5	7	28	140	80	Capital
Rotterdam	7	1	nil	—	—	Port. Industrial
Stavanger	0·5	11	71	220	203	Port
Stockholm	9·5	85	695	189	201	Capital
Stuttgart	5	27	290	132	168	Industrial
Turin	7	2	nil	6	—	Industrial
Zürich	4	86	946	476	682	Tourist

Sources: *Bradshaw International Air Guide U.N. Population Statistics*
ICAO Digest of Statistics

* 1954

external connections. Column (*a*) gives the population for the city named—to the nearest hundred thousand in the table. In order to establish a relationship between population and services available, some index is required to express the relation. In the table, fourteen 'sample' cities were taken at random and the number of services per million head of population calculated from the information in columns (*a*) and (*b*). The mean of these figures was calculated and taken as the base index of services generated per million head of population, and expressed as 100. Thus any particular city that generated more services than the mean rate for its size would show an index greater than 100. The indices that result are plotted in column (*d*) of the table, and referred to as the 'Service Index'.

Such an index has severe limitations and a further analysis was made using the total seats available per day on all routes in both directions at each city. This is a more accurate measurement of traffic, although still with some reservations. Column (*c*) plots the seats available, and column (*e*) plots the 'capacity index'. The latter is related to city size as before and is calculated in an analogous manner to that employed with the service index. Thus an index figure of more than 100 in column (*e*) indicates that the city's daily seat capacity is greater than the mean value for its size, while a figure less than 100 indicates a capacity below the mean.

The final column (*f*) indicates the oustanding functions of the city. More will be said on this point at a later stage.

A study of the indices—especially the capacity indices— indicates that size is not the only criterion of traffic. London is an example of a city that generates traffic more than in proportion to its size, while Naples is conspicuous in the other direction. From a map, Naples' position with relation to Rome suggests that it is overshadowed by the close proximity of that city, i.e. it is in a 'traffic shadow'. London's importance as a capital, market and route focus undoubtedly accounts for its high index. In other examples—e.g. Amsterdam and Brussels—proximity does not produce a traffic shadow and here the political separation of the two cities is more relevant. Industrial cities like Newcastle, Lyons or Turin, none of which appear overshadowed by adjacent cities, do not produce traffic on any great scale. Where industry is allied to other functions—e.g. Düsseldorf—the position is very different.

So far, then, we may distinguish the following relevant elements—size, proximity to other large cities, function and a 'strategic' site (or route focus). We may now consider each in more detail.

The importance of the size of a city may be easily demonstrated. If all towns served by airlines in Europe be taken—*Table XXX* represents a selection only—then of the seats availabe per day at all towns, the 'millionaire' (population > 1 million) cities of Western Europe, as listed above, account for 43% of the total. London and Paris alone account for 23·5%. On the other hand, of course, the cities with a population of less than a million account for 57%, but there are 38 of them involved. These figures show that size is an important consideration, but that it is not the only one may be seen by inspection of *Table XXX*. Birmingham, Naples and Vienna do not generate the capacity their size would lead us to expect, while smaller towns like Geneva, Nice and Zürich generate far more capacity than their size warrants.

After size we may next consider position. The distance between cities is a very relevant factor. In the first place, short intercity distances usually bring problems of surface competition. Secondly, where distances are less than 200 miles, the fixed-wing aircraft operates under unfavourable conditions, chiefly because so much time is spent taking-off and landing, and because the time taken to reach the airport from the city centre is a large proportion of the total travelling time. Finally, where cities are closely clustered, there is a tendency for one of them to become the traffic focus, while the remainder are handicapped by this fact—i.e. they are in a 'traffic shadow'. It will be realized that this last point is closely bound up with the first, for if surface links are good, then the tendency for one city to dominate will be expedited. Since European cities are closely spaced (*Table XXI*), and surface communications are good, we would expect traffic shadow to be important. At first sight such a characteristic does not seem to be well marked. Birmingham and Manchester operate to some extent under the shadow of London, Naples appears to be blanketed by Rome. Two cities included in *Table XXX* do not carry scheduled services at all, but have been included to show that size alone is no criterion. The cities involved are Turin and Rotterdam. Rotterdam is situated close to an important 'airline' town—Amsterdam—and is at least partly in that city's shadow. Turin, on the other hand, is not so placed, and traffic shadow is unlikely from Rome. So far our comparisons have been between towns that are served by scheduled airlines—with the exception of Turin and Rotterdam. The latter lead us to consider the matter in more detail, for they may not be the only cases.

As a more intensive example, we may take the area from Groningen to Paris and consider traffic shadow in relation to all towns over 100,000 population in that zone. *Table XXXI* shows the result—23 towns with more than 100,000 population (1962), of which only five appear on the airline schedules. Of these five, only Paris, Brussels and Amsterdam are important, Antwerp

TABLE XXXI

TOWNS WITH MORE THAN 100,000 POPULATION (1962)
IN THE GRONINGEN–PARIS AREA

	Population
Amsterdam	866,830*
Rotterdam	730,963*†
The Hague	604,112
Utrecht	261,043
Eindhoven	174,612
Haarlem	171,009
Groningen	149,486
Tilburg	141,580
Nijmegen	136,111
Enschede	130,256
Arnhem	127,955
Breda	113,193
Hilversum	103,310
Brussels	1,029,693*†
Antwerp	251,419†
Ghent	156,499
Liege	153,183†
Paris	2,790,091*
Lille	193,096*
Rheims	133,914
Rouen	120,857
Roubaix	112,856
Amiens	105,433

*Towns served by scheduled airline
†Helicopter Service

having a very low capacity index. Of great interest is the fact that four cities are served by helicopter. The three main traffic generators—Paris, Brussels and Amsterdam—are all closely spaced:

$$\text{Paris–Brussels (stage length)} = 156 \text{ st. miles}$$
$$\text{Brussels–Amsterdam} = 104 \text{ st. miles}$$

and it appears superfluous that three cities within such a small space should all be important. The key to the answer lies in the simple fact that each is in a different state. Two are capitals and the third is the main commercial city of the country (Amsterdam).

This more detailed survey represents a more accurate picture of size and traffic shadow in Europe. The area chosen represents the most densely populated area of the continent and highlights the position most strongly, and it is probable that no other area of comparable size would exhibit such a striking picture. Each of the cities within this belt is within overnight reach of surface transport, and competition from road and rail plays its part both in discouraging air traffic between the majority of the settlements, and also in confirming the importance of the focal cities of Brussels, Paris and Amsterdam.

If one now widens the net somewhat by considering the area that may be reached from each of these focal cities by overnight train service, we may delimit their orbits of influence more completely. Thus from London, the whole of the British Isles and the continental area west of a line through Stavanger, Rotterdam and Paris may be reached. If Paris is included, virtually the whole of Western Europe is accessible, although in detail individual services show wide variation. Within this zone, rail competition is likely to be most severe. The fact that most of the denser air routes come within the zone shows the size of the total traffic involved and not the incapacity of road and rail to compete, as *Table XXXII* shows. Perhaps the most illuminating fact concerns the relationship of London with the continental cities; in particular, the relationship of London and Paris. Both day and overnight rail services are available between these cities, yet the air traffic density on the air route between them is the highest in Europe. Such a picture cannot be ascribed solely to the total volume of traffic available. The need for transhipment on the surface—in spite of 'through sleeper' services by ferry—still tells

TABLE XXXII

DOMESTIC RAIL AND AIR PASSENGER KILOMETRES IN 1962
FOR SELECTED EUROPEAN COUNTRIES

	Rail Passengers Kms. (millions)	*Air Passengers Kms. (Scheduled Services) (millions)*
United Kingdom	31,820	1,312
France	35,800	1,281
Belgium	8,068	—
Netherlands	7,878	21
Switzerland	8,741	22

Sources: United Nations
ICAO

against the railway. It seems that people just do not like 'being messed about' by the necessity for shunting off and on steamer ferries. In short, London cannot be considered within the orbit of Paris, Brussels or Amsterdam, or vice versa. The English Channel must be held partly responsible for the fact that both London and Paris can exist as major traffic terminals, despite the fact that only some 219 miles separate them.

In summary, therefore, size is important, but surface competition, position, distance and political separation all modify the picture. Traffic shadow is manifest, in fact many large cities are affected by the phenomenon, but in detail no two areas appear completely analogous. The above summary has been brief and somewhat crude, and it must be admitted that a great deal of research is required before we can present a complete analysis—a task for which the geographer is surely well suited.

The next step is to consider the capacity indices of cities that are not obviously affected by traffic shadow, but which show marked 'size abnormality'. From *Table XXX* (and omitting German cities) Geneva, Nice, Zürich and Göteborg show high indices. Oslo and Copenhagen are likewise marked. Geneva and Zürich, only 150 miles apart and in the same state, are particularly noticeable. It has already been suggested that a capital city has an advantage derived from its function as such. Oslo and Copenhagen undoubtedly derive importance from their status as capitals. Function is also important in the case of the other cities mentioned above. Nice, in particular, derives enormous benefit from its function as a tourist centre, while Zürich and Geneva must likewise owe a great deal to Switzerland's popularity as a tourist centre. Geneva, as the old home of the League of Nations and at present the seat of many bodies associated with UNO, has come to be regarded as an 'International City'. This specialized function, too, has had its repercussions on air transport, for the constant flow of officials and delegates provides an obvious source of airline business. Göteborg, on the other hand, displays no marked function in the same sense as Nice, for example. Much of its importance is derived from its position as an intermediate point between continental Europe south of the Baltic and Scandinavia. Lying outside the orbit of any of the other important European cities, its position marks it as a regional centre in its own right.

If we now look at the capacity indices for other cities not affected by a traffic shadow, but this time marked by a low index, we may pick out Turin, Lyons and Lisbon. These three display no common function, but it is of interest to note that both Lyons and Turin are important industrial centres. Lisbon, as an important staging point on Atlantic routes, ought to be in a position very different from the picture given by the capacity index. A hint of the answer is given by comparing the service and capacity index for Lisbon. Thus a large number of cities are served from Lisbon, but the traffic generated is low. Such characteristics suggest a city that handles a variety of traffic 'staging through', but generates very little of its own. Lisbon, situated in a predominantly agricultural area away from the main industrial centres of population, but with a strategic position in relation to Atlantic routes, seems just such a city. Its tourist attraction does not markedly affect the situation.

Capital cities have already revealed their importance, but the smaller regional capitals must also be remembered. In a continent of short distances and varied political conditions, the regional capital is not easily picked out from the standpoint of air traffic, since so many possible cases are overshadowed by adjacent cities, but Düsseldorf as a centre for the Ruhr, and Hamburg for north Germany, are two cases that might well be investigated. Göteborg has already been alluded to, while British towns like Birmingham and Bristol seem well within the traffic shadow of London. Glasgow displays characteristics more akin to those of Lisbon than Düsseldorf or Hamburg. Glasgow's industrial activities seem to account for little—an interesting parallel with Turin. Lyons is completely anomalous, with a capacity index of only 9 in 1954.

One final observation seems appropriate. The strategic position of certain cities on important trunk air routes—particularly extra-European—has been manifest, e.g. London and Paris, perhaps the supreme examples. The importance of this aspect cannot be readily perceived in the case of these two cities, since they derive importance from so many other elements. That strategic position should not be over-rated is best seen with respect to Lisbon and Glasgow. It will be seen that all cities that occupy such positions display a high service indes in *Table XXX*, which is not an unreasonable result.

A sample network : British European Airways

So far we have considered European air transport in terms of routes and cities; we may now consider the matter from the standpoint of an individual network. BEA has been chosen mainly because of its size, but also because of the excellent statistical material available concerning its operations.[2] To place the airline in its right perspective, we must first look at some figures dealing with European airlines as a whole. *Table XXXIII* shows the proportion of daily seat miles supplied by the leading airlines, together with the passenger load factor achieved on their operations. *Table XXXIV* shows the achieved passenger load factor for some of the British independent operators for comparison. It is apparent that BEA is one of the larger and more successful airlines, with a high load factor in relation to the short stages it must work. In a broader context, it is notable that most of the traffic is concentrated into the hands of the top eight operators. With some exceptions, their load factors are not very high, and when the independent operators are added it can be seen that the efficiency of European airlines, as judged by load factors alone, is not outstanding.

The figures suggest that, whereas the major airlines appear moderately efficient, the smaller operators on the scheduled air routes of UK registration are 'too many chasing too few passenger miles'. In *Table XXXIV*, the high load factor of some operators was achieved on one or two routes only.

TABLE XXXIII

DAILY SEAT/MILES AND ACHIEVED LOAD FACTORS
OF THE LEADING WEST EUROPEAN AIRLINES

(Seat mileage 1961. L/F 1963)

Airline	% total daily seat/miles*	L/F on international operations†	L/F on domestic operations
BEA	23	60	70
Air France	18	51	66
SAS	11	49	56 Denmark
			62 Norway
			54 Sweden
Alitalia	8	45	65
Swissair	7	53	56
KLM	7	44	—
Lufthansa	7	53	56
Iberia	5	44	71
Sabena	5	46	—
Olympic	4	54	64
Aer Lingus	3	67	51
Finnair	3	49	59

* Refers to intra-European and domestic services only
† Includes all international operations

Sources: *ICAO Digest of Statistics*

Returning to BEA, the first point of interest concerns the shape of the network operated. Most networks are variations on three major themes—a 'spoke' or 'star' pattern of routes, a 'grid', or a 'linear' pattern. BEA, in common with the other major European operators, has a spoke-route pattern with its centre at London and its extremities stretching from Oslo and Stockholm in the north through Berlin, Vienna and the eastern Mediterranean to Lisbon, Belfast and the Shetlands. That such a shape is so characteristic of European conditions may be easily seen. Each political unit operates its own network outwards from the capital to all, or most, of the other leading European centres, usually through bilateral agreements. Europe's compact shape, and the number of states involved, results in a series of interlocking spoke networks with the capitals (or major cities in some cases—e.g. Amsterdam) as the nodal points. Some networks will be 'skew', according to the position of the individual state concerned. Thus

TABLE XXXIV

ACHIEVED PASSENGER LOAD FACTORS:
BRITISH INDEPENDENT OPERATORS 1963

Operator	% L/F international scheduled services	% L/F domestic services
Air Ferry	66	—
BKS	57	68
British Eagle	60	16
British United	40	79
B.U. Air Ferries	44	13
Cambrian	59	65
Channel Airways	58	58
Dan Air	19	50
Derby	71	66
Jersey	57	62
Morton	38	66
Silver City	49	64
Skyways	50	—
Starways	79	62

Source: *ICAO Digest of Statistics, Traffic*

Scandinavian networks show a strong bias to the west and south. BEA, with important connections to Europe and a strong domestic network radiating northwards from London, shows a more complete radial pattern.

Such a pattern brings certain advantages and disadvantages to its operator. On the credit side must be accounted the possibility of centralized maintenance services at the hub of the network—i.e. London in BEA's case—since most aircraft will operate to and from the hub. The control of aircraft movements is simplified and since the control of schedules is a prime necessity, this is a distinct advantage. Similarly, the sales side of the business is aided by the presence of a central node.

On the other hand, a spoke pattern brings certain difficulties. Aircraft and crew utilization is difficult to rationalize, since each extremity of the network is isolated from its neighbour and machines must return directly. Furthermore, the stage lengths are short, so that each individual route is not long enough to warrant 'crew slipping' en route. Apart from the hub station, traffic flow through each of the other points is low and this tends to make station costs proportionately higher than they would be with a more even and bigger flow. Finally, weather can be a vital consideration at the hub airport, for, since the majority of routes start and finish at this point, bad weather at the hub will affect most of the airline's schedules. Should the hub be important to other operators—including those staging through—weather conditions will be even more important. London's position as a major route focus is a case in point. With short stage lengths making ground time a vital issue, prolonged 'stacking' at the hub airport in bad weather can add appreciably to the time of the air section of a journey made on BEA's routes.

From the network as a whole, we may now turn to the individual components. The basic division is into international and domestic routes. In the case of BEA the latter are, with some exceptions, the shorter group in terms of stage length. The variation in stage length, taking all routes operated, is from twenty-four miles (Guernsey–Jersey) to 1,086 miles (London–Gibraltar). The average stage length operated on the domestic network (including Channel Island Services) is 155 miles, while for international routes the figure is 459 miles. In terms of traffic, four domestic routes were included in the six most important routes operated in 1954–55, an indication of their status in the network as a whole.

In more detail, BEA's routes demonstrate the features already shown to be characteristic of European conditions. Over-water stages are an important element on both domestic and international operations. (*Table XXXV*.) If one takes the twenty-seven busiest routes, twenty of them involve a water crossing, and of the remainder, four are internal German operations, and three are domestic routes between London, Glasgow, Manchester and Edinburgh. Perhaps the most surprising feature is the position of the domestic routes so near the top of the list, in spite of the fact that most involve stage lengths of less than 250 miles. A comparison between the 1954–55 and 1963–64 figures in *Table XXXV* shows the ascendancy of the leading pair of domestic routes between the two periods. BEA account for the increase partly as the result of greater domestic traffic, and partly as the result of a substantial increase in the number of passengers travelling to London for connection with long-distance services. The latter aspect reflects the advantage BEA reaps from its use of London Airport—one of the major foci in Europe. The purely domestic traffic is a more interesting case, for rail competition might be

TABLE XXXV

LEADING BEA ROUTES: 1954–55 AND 1963–64

Route	Passengers Carried 1954–55
London–Paris	235,430
London–Jersey	126,189
London–Glasgow	92,347
London–Belfast	77,877
Berlin–Hanover	72,798
Glasgow–Belfast	48,366
London–Düsseldorf	45,831
Berlin–Hamburg	45,126
London–Guernsey	42,611
London–Manchester	41,684
London–Nice	41,254
London–Zurich	40,907
	1963–64
London–Glasgow	500,000
London–Manchester	383,000
London–Paris	379,000

Sources: *BEA Report and Accounts 1954–55*
Flight International

expected to be intense over these short routes. In April 1954, too, BEA increased most of its domestic fares by 5–10% although, even with the increase, domestic fares were still generally as much as 25% below the average rate per passenger mile on its international services.

Without an analysis of passenger 'types', it is difficult to ascertain which class of traveller actually used the domestic routes. Business traffic undoubtedly forms the hard core—particularly between the commercial and financial centres in London and the industrial towns of the north. Such traffic presumably does not show great seasonal fluctuation. Tourist movements are obviously the mainstay of many routes, e.g. London–Guernsey, and seasonal differences are here more acute. That many routes involve a water crossing should not be forgotten, especially those routes that span the Irish Sea, where a crossing by steamer ferry can be most upsetting!*

* Liverpool–Isle of Man by sea takes 4 hours; by air takes 40 minutes (2 hours from London to Isle of Man).

The fact that domestic traffic has increased is noteworthy, for with increased traffic the use of bigger aircraft at a higher utilization rate becomes more feasible, and with it a reduction of operating costs. Just how far such progress may be made with fixed-wing aircraft on short-stage lengths where ground time is so important is problematical. Much has been written to show that Britain's domestic network is an ideal one for the large commercial helicopter. BEA's experimental services with this type of machine stretch back to its mail service in 1948,[5] since which time it has constantly maintained its interest. In June 1954 it opened the world's first scheduled passenger service with a British helicopter from London Airport to Eastleigh (Southampton), maintaining a regularity of 96% over the summer months and carrying 700 passengers during the period. The most recent service, opened in 1964, uses S 61–N helicopters to replace fixed-wing aircraft on the Scilly Isles service.

That no widespread adoption of helicopters has taken place is due to the state of development of the machine itself. BEA have suggested their requirements on several occasions (*Table XXXVI*), but neither the 'Rotodyne' nor the 'BEA line bus' has materialised. Indeed, the modern idea of an 'airbus' is a large, economical, fixed-wing aircraft.

One final aspect of the domestic network is worthy of special mention. The Scottish routes operating between Renfrew

TABLE XXXVI

HELICOPTER PERFORMANCE: PRESENT AND FUTURE

Type	Cruising speed (m.p.h.)	Seating capacity	Economic sector distance at full load (statute miles)
Bristol 171 Mk. 3A	90–95	4	59
Westland WS 55 (BEA)	72–101	5	103
Bristol 173 Mk. 3	138	16	230*
BEA 1951 Specification	138	30	115
Fairey Rotodyne†	150	40–50	250*
Projected 'BEA line Bus'	160	48–64	200

* Estimated   † Under construction

AIRCRAFT COSTS PER SEAT/MILE FOR HELICOPTERS AND
FIXED-WING AIRCRAFT

(2,000-hour p.a. utilization)

Type	Pence per seat/mile, for stage distance (miles				
	50	100	150	200	250
HELICOPTERS:					
Bristol 171	14·0	12·0	—	—	—
Bristol 173 Mk. 1	10·0	9·5	11·0	13·0	—
Mk. 3	6·0	5·3	5·5	6·4	—
BEAline Bus	4·0	3·3	3·4	3·6	4·0
FIXED-WING:					
DC–3 'Pionair'	5·0	3·0	2·6	2·2	2·0
Viscount V–701	5·0	2·8	2·0	1·9	1·8

Sources: *BEA Report and Accounts*; *Flight*, 1953, 1955;
'Thoughts on the Future of the Transport Helicopter',
P. G. Masefield, Lecture to Helicopter Association of
Great Britain, November 1952

(Glasgow) and the outlying islands of the Hebrides, Orkneys and
Shetlands represent an example of 'social' services, for they do not
generate sufficient traffic to make them economically self-support-
ing. Here, the difficulties of surface transport make the air link a
vital asset to the islanders. Not only are passenger services run,
but mail and freight and a special ambulance service are included.
Table XXXVII illustrates the value of the latter service, and this
aspect alone justifies the continuance of the network. The short
sectors and poor airfield facilities make this section of BEA's
network a special case. Aircraft like the De Havilland 'Heron'
and the H.P. 'Herald' suited to operation from small airfields are
employed, and it is not without significance that Scotland's only
aircraft manufacturer—Scottish Aviation Ltd.—should have
built the 'Pioneer' and 'Twin-Pioneer' machines, both designed
specifically for operation in difficult terrain. The 'Pioneer's' success
in the jungles of Malaysia points to the progress made in this
direction. Many think that such machines will be of more use
under the difficult conditions of routes like the Scottish examples
than the somewhat temperamental helicopter.

The magnitude of BEA's international traffic may be judged

TABLE XXXVII

SCOTTISH AIR AMBULANCE SERVICE

Period	No. of Flights	Patients carried	Mileage
1933–42	540	600*	150,000*
1944	59	70	20,000*
1948	245	285	67,635
1950	240	290	57,175
1954	274	320	59,020
1963–64	283	341	60,828

Cost of service borne by the National Health Service since 1948

* Estimated

Sources: *Flight*, April 1955
         BEA

by the fact that in 1954–55 the airline carried more than a million passengers—the second highest international total for any airline in the world at that time. In 1963–64 the figure had reached 3,021,222 passengers. When domestic traffic is added, the figure is more than $5\frac{1}{2}$ million. Tourist fares, introduced in 1953, have undoubtedly helped towards the increase in traffic and made the utilization of BEA's new aircraft more economic. In addition, seasonal peaks have shown a decrease in magnitude, attributed by the airline to an increase of winter traffic and the introduction of night services (*Table XXXVIII*). Part of the increase in winter

TABLE XXXVIII

SEASONAL TRAFFIC TRENDS: BEA

Revenue Passengers carried (scheduled passengers services)

Year	Peak months (August)	Lowest traffic month (February)
1951–52	163,112	51,142
1952–53	205,424	67,815 (Jan. 1953)
1953–54	248,331	73,305
1954–55	255,000	89,000
1963–64	691,598	297,310

Source: *BEA Report and Accounts*

traffic is accounted for by business travellers and part by the increase in winter sports tourists.

The routes themselves call for little comment over that already given for European routes in general. Cross-channel routes are outstanding, with London–Paris by far the most important single example from the point of view of traffic. Tourist traffic to the French and Swiss resorts is conspicuous, while internal German services still rank high on the list.

Freight traffic, in comparison to passenger traffic, is far less important and showed no marked development until 1960; since when the average annual increase in traffic has been between 15 and 20%. Although all-cargo routes are offered by BEA, 63% of the freight traffic handled was carried on passenger services. Seasonal variations in freight traffic are far less marked, and this, too, is an important feature.

In conclusion, two points should be emphasized. In the first place, on a network like that of BEA, it is vitally important that the aircraft used should 'fit the job'. In the future we may see the airline operating aircraft as diverse as the Hawker Siddeley 'Trident', the 'Argosy' freighter, helicopters and, perhaps, the large 'airbus', each suited to particular routes on BEA's short-range but varied network. Secondly, the importance of the city-airport ground link cannot be over-emphasized. BEA's new city terminal at Cromwell Road, Kensington, linked through the Cromwell Road extension to London Airport, is still hampered by congestion on the roads, although M4 is now available for traffic.

Table XXXIX summarises some of the more important aspects of the airline's work for the year 1963–64.

Air freight in Europe. A sample survey

At present no detailed analysis of the air cargo traffic of European airlines is possible, since figures relating to the origin and destination of cargoes are not available on a representative scale. *Table XL* shows the proportion of total revenue accounted for by freight traffic on BEA's routes. Not only is the proportion very low, but the trend in recent years has been downwards. The chief reason for this appears to be due to the introduction of tourist fares in 1953. In that year the free baggage allowance was reduced and the excess baggage revenue figures showed an increase of £154,194 over 1952–53. The restoration of the free allowance

TABLE XXXIX

BRITISH EUROPEAN AIRWAYS: LEADING STATISTICS
(1963–64)

	International services (million)	Domestic services (million)	Total (million)
TRAFFIC:			
Capacity ton/miles offered	278·3	100·5	378·8
Load ton/miles sold	163·4	63·7	227·1
Revenue Load Factor (%)	58·7	63·4	60·0
Revenue passengers carried	3·0	2·6	5·6
Passenger miles flown	1,354·9	638·7	1,993·6
Available seat/miles	2,219·2	925·2	3,144·3
Passenger Load Factor (%)	61·1	69·0	63·4
Mail ton/miles	3·7	1·7	5·4
Freight ton/miles	19·0	3·9	22·9
OPERATIONS:			
Unduplicated Route miles	33,342	2,851	36,193
Revenue hours flown	114,212	51,199	165,411
Total no. revenue flights	74,406	58,259	132,665
Aircraft miles (millions)	29·3	10·3	39·6
Passenger flights operated	68,103	55,750	123,853
Passenger service regularity (%)	97·8	95·8	96·9
Average flight duration (minutes)	92	53	75
Average length of flight (statute miles)	394	177	299
Average distances carried (statute miles):			
Passengers	448	247	356
Mail	556	265	413
Freight	471	217	393

Source: BEA Report and Accounts 1963–64

in 1954–55 resulted in a reversal of the trend in the excess baggage revenue, the figure being £107,599 less than for the previous year (12% decrease). Even allowing for these changes on the total passenger revenue, it is still manifest that tourist fares have increased the importance of passenger revenue.

TABLE XL

BEA REVENUE ANALYSIS

	% of Total Revenue				
	1951–52	*1952–53*	*1953–54*	*1954–55*	*1963–64*
Passenger	80·0	81·2	83·3	86·0	89·8
Mail	8·7	9·0	8·2	7·9	3·4
Freight	11·3	9·8	8·5	6·1	6·8

Source: *BEA Reports and Accounts*

Most freight is carried on the passenger services, forming a 'fill-up' cargo for the aircraft. Some 37% of the freight carried goes by international all-cargo service. Freight traffic, therefore, faces a number of difficulties, for in order to make the specialized cargo route worthwhile, a large increase in traffic is required. At the same time, the increase in passenger traffic has meant an increase in cargo space on the aircraft used for these services. Cargo rates are lower than the passenger equivalents, and so not only is more space available on mixed traffic machines, but any attempt to reduce rates and attract traffic would be difficult. The use of large air freighters has improved the freight situation, but such machines cannot be expected to be effective unless the traffic available to them is sufficiently large to make possible the economies of a high utilization rate.

The amount of freight carried on passenger services varies with the route. *Table XLI* shows four samples and plots the proportion of the payload represented by freight shipments. The variation suggests that city function again has relevance, together with the usual route characteristics of distance and terrain type covered. A much wider study is needed before we can be certain of any correlation, but the figures suggest that industrial and commercial cities, particularly those separated by water, are the more important. Tourist routes show the smallest percentage.

The seasonal characteristics of freight traffic have already been alluded to ; briefly, freight traffic does not show the violent summer peaks of passenger movements, while the tendency for mid-week shipments counteracts the week-end peaks of passenger traffic. Whereas tourist traffic has tended to increase the seasonal differences, it has also provided the operator with another

TABLE XLI

PROPORTION OF FREIGHT CARRIED ON SAMPLE PASSENGER
SERVICES. MARCH 1954

Airline	Air-craft	Route	No. of Flights	Total payload carried* (tonnes)	Freight (tonnes)	Freight as % of total payload
KLM	Convair 240	Amsterdam–Manchester	9	20·92	5·83	28
Swissair	"	London–Geneva	31	49·83	2·53	2
Air France	V–708	London–Paris	155	445·5	53·6	12
BEA	V–701	London–Palma	10	33·7	nil	—

Source: *ICAO.*, *Digest of Statistics*

* To calculate total payload carried, 10 passengers assumed=1 tonne

possibility. Since tourist passengers do not receive the same degree of comfort as the standard-rate passengers, higher density seating is possible on the aircraft used. In this way, the proportion of unwanted cargo space may possibly be reduced. Larger aircraft —e.g. Vickers 'Vanguard'—may operate either as mixed traffic machines carrying standard passenger accommodation and freight, or as high density passenger aircraft with more limited freight accommodation. The large freight holds specified for the 'Vanguard' makes available considerable freight capacity when required. Any final separation of function into all-freight and all-passenger types must await a far greater increase in freight traffic and an evening-up of the seasonal passenger movements.

The type of commodity carried is shown in *Table XII*, but little information exists on the origin and destination of such cargoes, for not only are scheduled services involved, but also a considerable proportion of charter shipments. That charter operations are an essential element in air freighting results from the nature of the traffic. Most freight is carried only one way and becomes available at irregular intervals in many instances. In order to demonstrate the nature of charter work, we may consider some examples. *Table XLII* shows some sample charter operations and illustrates the importance of freight traffic.

TABLE XLII

CHARTER OPERATIONS: BRITISH INDEPENDENT OPERATORS

	Load Ton Miles (thousands)	Freight Ton Miles (thousands)	Freight as % of Total Payload
1957–58	95,150	48,522	50·5
1959–60	104,872	56,836	54·2
1961–62	102.910	44,835	43·6
1962–63	110,912	19,919	18·0

Source: *B.I.A.T.A. Annual Report*

These examples again demonstrate the significance of over-water routes and the saving that results in the use of air transport.

Packaging of goods sent by air need only be a fraction of that necessary for rail or sea transport. In some cases the saving in cost can more than offset the higher cost of the air fare. During the dock strike in the UK in 1956, one engineering firm sent a delicate piece of machinery by air to the continent for the first time. The saving on packaging that resulted was £156, whereas the cost of sending the machine by air was £125.

Animals form a very common cargo on both charter and scheduled operations. The RSPCA Hostel at London Airport handles over 300,000 animals of all types a year, except giraffes, for which the aircraft designer has yet to produce a suitable aircraft! BEA carries a heavy traffic of goldfish from Bologna and dogs from all parts of Europe, while regular shipments of leeches for London hospitals are brought in from southern France. Much of the traffic is destined for overseas destinations, e.g. British bloodstock—from racehorses to Siamese cats—have appeared on cargo manifests, destined chiefly for the Americas and the Commonwealth.

Between November 1951 and March 1952, Silver City Airways received a contract to fly 1,800 live cattle across the Channel from Lympne to Le Touquet. This was part of a journey from Dublin to Italy, the remainder being carried out by sea and rail, i.e. :

> Dublin by sea to Liverpool
> Liverpool–Westerhanger (rail)
> Lympne–Le Touquet (air)
> Le Touquet–Italy (rail)

Each aircraft carried an average of eight animals per trip, with shipments totalling 800 per week. This represented a saving of more than a day on the transit time for each beast. Since it was calculated that a bullock loses 1·5% fat content in twenty-four hours when travelling, this represents a saving of 30,000–40,000 lb. of beef, or £10,000.

Finally, perishable goods, such as flowers and fruit, form another source of revenue for the freight operator. In season, strawberries flown into London from Verona are on sale twenty-four hours after they are picked—a saving of five days. The rate quoted for such shipments varies with the season, a typical figure works out at about 10d./lb., or less if a return cargo is available. Not only does the fruit arrive in better condition, but the necessity for a 'pipeline' of shipments is obviated and supplies may be quickly regulated according to market conditions. Daffodils are another cargo carried by charter operations. Each spring, thousands of buds are flown into London from the Scilly Isles, representing similar savings to the shipper and customer as in the case of fruit.

REFERENCES

1. Air Research Bureau. *Intra-European Air Passenger Traffic, 1952–54*. (Brussels, 1955.)
   Air Research Bureau. *Internal Transport in Europe*. (Brussels, 1953.)
2. British European Airways. *Report and Accounts* (Annual).
3. Fitzgerald, G. 'Passenger Survey', *Shell Aviation News*, 1955.
4. Hilgerdt, F. *The Network of World Trade*. (League of Nations, Geneva, 1942.)
5. Hislop, G. S. 'British European Airways Helicopter Unit', *Flight*, January 1953.
6. Wheatcroft, S. *The Economics of European Air Transport*. (Manchester, 1956.)
7. Wheatcroft, S. F. *Air Transport Policy*. Michael Joseph, 1964.

6

AIR TRANSPORT IN THE UNITED STATES

Introduction

North America, the third largest continent, presents a more simple ground plan than Europe. Three major political divisions account for 90% of the total area of some eight million square miles, while the USA and Canada between them have jurisdiction over 7,400,000 square miles (*Table XLIII*).

TABLE XLIII

STATE AREAS IN NORTH AMERICA

State	Area (sq. miles) Nearest thousand
Canada	3,700,000
USA*	3,738,000
Mexico	767,000
Central American States and British Honduras	240,000
	8,445,000

* Including Alaska and other non-contiguous territories

In size, the United States represents a sub-continental area roughly equal to that of Greater Europe (3,873,000 sq. mls.).

The boundaries of North America are easily defined since the continent is essentially an island. The United States, situated between the less hospitable lands of Canada and Mexico, has two land and two sea boundaries. The 'double ocean' aspect of

the USA is of great significance in trade and transport and contrasts with the peninsula of Europe. The land boundaries, although largely arbitrary, are nevertheless stable and well defined.

World position and physical setting of the USA

With Europe as the centre of the land hemisphere, Asia and
North America represent the two flanks. Before the aeroplane
this fact was of academic importance, since the presence of polar
ice gave a strong east–west component to trade routes. The
United States, with its boundaries on two oceans, reaped the
advantages of a double aspect and its position was at least as
favourable as that of Europe. The aeroplane has reasserted the
fundamental facts of the American continent's global position,
for its peripheral site, with respect to the disposition of the land
masses of the land hemisphere, must be taken as a disadvantage
in comparison with Europe. Thus, by sea, New York is nearer
Tokyo than London is (11,200 miles as compared with 12,700
miles), but by air the position is reversed (6,700 miles as compared
with 5,900 miles). *Table XX* gives some further comparative air
distances. The USA's position with respect to the land hemisphere
is directly analogous to that of the Asiatic USSR, or in other words
the USA lies north-south of Asia rather than east-west of it in
terms of the shortest distance.

From such considerations one might expect the principal air
routes serving the USA to show strong northerly or southerly
components. Traffic from Europe and Asia might be expected
to reach the country from Canada, Alaska and the two oceans
(through the gateways of the north-eastern states and the Pacific
north-west), while southwards, traffic to the remaining continents
would pass through the gateways of Florida and California.

In practice, this 'quadrantal' pattern of international routes is
somewhat modified by other factors. The greatest single anomaly
results from the absence of air routes between the USA and the
USSR and China. Thus the north-east passage from New York
is directed towards Europe (and Africa) only—the great North
Atlantic bridge. Transits to Moscow and cities east of that point
might be expected to show a greater northerly swing across the
polar regions than present Atlantic routes display. Similarly, the
north-west passage from Seattle to Alaska and the Far East is
restricted to traffic for Japan, South-east Asia and India. None
crosses into the Asiatic USSR and little reaches China.

The southward-flowing routes to Australasia and South America are, by contrast, nearer the expected pattern. Latin-American routes follow one or other of two well-defined directions. Part of the traffic leaves the USA through New Orleans, Houston or San Antonio and runs through Mexico City to Panama and South America, while the remainder leaves from New Orleans or Miami through the West Indies to Latin-American destinations. In addition a certain amount of traffic from San Diego and Los Angeles connects southwards to Mexico City. Routes to South America, therefore, show a considerable 'spread', although Miami is probably the greatest single gateway.

Routes to Australia and New Zealand leave the Pacific coast not only from Los Angeles, but from Seattle also, and break the journey at Honolulu, Canton Island, Suva and Noumea. Traffic on these routes is but a fraction of the South American examples.

The above case points to a further modification of the route pattern, resulting from the fact that the USA is flanked by two great oceans. Atlantic routes make use of the intermediate stops in Newfoundland, Greenland and Iceland to break up the long ocean crossing, and result in a southerly transit. The introduction of aircraft capable of making the crossing non-stop in 1956 focussed attention on the shorter great circle distances, insofar as they were compatible with pressure-pattern navigation requirements. The Pacific Ocean is different. The longer east–west crossing making use of the Pacific islands as transit points has long held the field. Difficult physical conditions, together with a poor coverage by radio aids and a lack of USSR traffic, have made the shorter great circle passage through Alaska less important. Like the Europe–USSR–Far East route, this one may yet assume its rightful place.

Within the USA itself, the greatest development of air routes has taken place. This domestic network is the main concern of this chapter. In character it is the nearest analogue to the inter-European network, but in contrast to the latter it is essentially a long- and medium-haul system and one, moreover, that has grown up under the jurisdiction of a single political authority. *Table XLIV* illustrates the stage lengths involved and may usefully be compared with *Table XXI*.

In outline the physical sub-division of the USA is simple: two mountain systems, the Western Cordillera and the Appalachians, separated by the variable relief of the Central Plains.

TABLE XLIV

AIRLINE DISTANCES BETWEEN AMERICAN CITIES

(Airport–airport distance. Statute miles)

New York–Chicago	724	Chicago–Los Angeles	1,751
„ „ –Washington	215	„ –San Francisco	1,856
„ „ –Miami	1,090	„ –Miami	1,186
„ „ –Detroit	511	„ –Washington	600
„ „ –St. Louis	811		
„ „ –Montreal	325		
„ „ –Houston	1,430	Seattle–Anchorage	1,446
„ „ –Seattle	2,620		
„ „ –San Francisco	2,580		
„ „ –Los Angeles	2,475		

From the point of view of accessibility, the outstanding fact is the almost north–south alignment of these physical elements, parallel to the coasts and across the main line of air mass movements. With the exception of the Great Lakes region, much of the USA lies beyond easy reach of tidewater. The only 'open' coast lies along the Gulf of Mexico, which with the Mississippi favours north-south movement. Since the predominant line of trade movement in the country is east-west, most traffic is across the natural grain of the continent.

In more detail, the Western Cordillera stands out as a region of sparse development separating the populous area east of the 100° meridian from the much narrower, but still important, Pacific coast. Only some half-dozen railroad routes traverse the Cordillera, but most carry a heavy traffic. The Appalachian mountains form far less of an obstruction, although rail and road concentrations occur in the natural gaps like the Mohawk, Susquehanna, Potomac or New Rivers. Even so, some railroads that cross the mountains—e.g. Pennsylvanian—carry as much traffic as some river gap lines, or even more. The densest surface network of all occurs in the plains and plateaux of the north-east industrial area[4] and the great crop belts of the mid-west.

Trans-continental traffic is supplemented by a well-developed coastal steamer system linking the east and west coasts through the Panama Canal. Of still greater importance is the coastal link from the Gulf to the Atlantic coast ports, much of the traffic being accounted for by tankers. The Great Lakes are of immense importance. Their part in the economic development of the country has been very great, and their strategic position with relation to the resources of the east and mid-west is of incalculable value. In contrast, the Mississippi is a distinct hindrance to east–west movement. Until recently, only one railroad crossing existed between Memphis and New Orleans—a distance of some 400 miles.

Climate is also affected by the north–south structural grain. Some of the effects of the Western Cordillera on jet streams were discussed at an earlier stage, but the mountains exert an influence of much wider significance. *Fig. 5* shows the percentage occurrence of Contact Flying Weather in the USA and one is immediately struck by the differences between the Pacific coast and the interior. Since air masses reach the coast from the Pacific, low cloud is prevalent on the narrow coast plains and on the windward slopes of the Coastal and Cascade Ranges due to orographic effect. In addition the cold Californian Current over which air masses must move to reach the coast produces fog in the San Francisco district. Many weather regimes characterize the west coast, from the arid south to the oceanic climate of the north-west. The windward slopes of the Rockies again produce low cloud conditions. The inter-montane plateaux and the western plains show, by contrast, a high percentage of contact flying weather. In the arid south-western districts, almost perfect flying weather occurs for some 350 days of the year—one reason why the great Edwards test base is situated in this area.

Over the mid-western plains weather is not nearly as settled as it has been painted, for the passage of depressions disrupts the continental high pressure system in winter and convectional instability may bring poor flying weather in summer. The fact that the Central Lowlands are open to the Gulf in the south results in considerable influence from this zone penetrating the interior. Much of the interior's summer rainfall results from Gulf influence. Tornadoes, too, may penetrate the interior from the south as well as affecting the Atlantic coast states. The Great Lakes modify climatic conditions in the north-east, particularly as they form with the St. Lawrence a marked cyclone track.

The eastern USA again shows variability. The Appalachians unlike the Western Cordillera, are not high enough to prevent Atlantic influence reaching the interior, nor do they prevent climatic influences from the Gulf from reaching the central states. The north-east states, adjacent to the cyclone track of the Great Lakes and St. Lawrence and influenced by the Atlantic and the smoke of their own cities, are another zone of variable flying weather conditions.

Air transport has to contend, then, with a wider range of weather conditions than one finds in Europe. All conditions, from those of poor visibility, icing and turbulence, to near perfect weather are encountered. Only the tropical regimes are missing and even these are approached in the extreme south. Whereas climate undoubtedly affects surface transport, particularly in the western half of the continent, sheer distance is probably more generally important. The wide climatic range also makes available great possibilities for tourism, and resorts as far apart as the west coast and Florida are significant to the airline operator.

Population and market potential

From a study of *Tables XVI, XVII* and *XVIII* the general importance of the USA may be readily seen. Although the whole of North America accounts for only some 9% of the world's population, it actually generates some 40% of the total world income and has the highest *per capita* income in the world. The dominant position of the United States is suggested in *Table XVI*, and in economic terms represents an enormous potential market for air transport services.

Population distribution shows a marked pattern in the USA. In the north-east, the industrial regions form the nuclei of an area of dense population stretching from Chicago and Cincinnati to the Atlantic seaboard. Around this quadrant of the country lie the populated states of the Mid-West, Atlantic coast and the South. Together, these form the more densely populated eastern half of the continent. West of the great crop belts, population thins out rapidly in the High Plains and the Cordillera before the smaller zones of denser population are reached on the Pacific coast. Here, three main centres are visible: the Los Angeles region, the Central Valley of California, and the Seattle–Willamette lowlands. The first two are confined to a narrow coastal strip, but the last extends up the Columbia to the Palouse country around Spokane. Perhaps the most significant feature of this pattern, from our point of view, is the great 'gap' represented by the mountain States, separating the older established centres of the east from the growing cities of the far west.

Urban concentrations are also important elements. The closely spaced cities of the north-east resemble the European pattern and are most likely to raise short-stage problems to air transport operators. Beyond this region, cities are far more widely spaced. At this point we might just note the chain of mid-continental cities stretching from Minneapolis and St. Paul in the north, through Omaha, Kansas City, St. Louis, Memphis and Dallas, to the gulf coast towns from Houston to Mobile. Beyond this belt, large towns become even more widely separated as one moves west, but Great Falls, Denver, Salt Lake City, Albuquerque and El Paso are noteworthy as stepping-stones on the road west-wards. Finally, there remain the cities of the Pacific coast, with Los Angeles, San Francisco, Portland and Seattle outstanding. The need for rapid trans-continental communications suggests that all these cities are likely to loom large in the domestic pattern of us air routes.

Potential passenger traffic is here, as in Europe, the greatest source of revenue. Once again the north-east represents the biggest potential market with New York and Chicago the great foci of the area (*Fig. 10*). These two cities generate more traffic than any others in the United States. Into and out of this core run the main trade routes, linking the eastern industries with the great agricultural regions of the Mid-West and the South, and the growing industrial regions of Texas and the Pacific coast. Business traffic carried by the airlines follows a similar east–west, and to a smaller degree north–south, pattern staging through the cities of the mid-continent. Perhaps the most suitable field for air trans-port lies in the trans-continental connections where sheer distance tells against its surface competitors. In addition, the populated east is separated from the cities of the west coast by the mountains, plateaux and basins of the Cordillera and High Plains.

Unlike the European scene, distance is of great importance. Thus the great domestic carriers do not provide anything like as intensive a network as is possible within the smaller confines of Western Europe. These facts are undoubtedly one reason for the rise of a phenomenon almost unknown in Europe—the develop-ment of the business executive aircraft owned and operated by individual companies and corporations for their own use. Such aircraft now account for approximately 60% of all business traffic in the usa.[5] By 1953 general aviation business transportation accounted for 1,000,000 more flying hours than were flown by the scheduled carriers. For the scheduled airline, therefore, competition arises not only from surface transport, but also from private and business-owned machines. One further point is noteworthy in this connection. Most of the post-war industrial expansion has occurred outside the 550 towns and cities served by the scheduled carriers.

Tourist traffic is difficult to assess, but both summer and winter travel is important. The Canadian and US western mountain resorts cater for summer visitors, but also represent centres for winter sports. Southern resorts, of which Miami and Palm Beach are outstanding, are examples of winter resorts, particularly for northern visitors. Again, summer traffic is also a feature. The sunshine and mountain scenery of the south-western states represent tourist assets utilized by such all-season resorts as Las Vegas and Phoenix. Tradition plays its part in certain places, perhaps the best example being Niagara Falls—the Mecca of honeymoon couples.

The movement of cargo by air is a growing part of the air transport picture. Domestic airlines obtain about 7% of their revenue from freight shipments. Although regular freight operations were carried out before 1941, the war demonstrated the possibilities and provided a training ground for the enormous post-war growth. At present three regular all-freight airlines are certificated by the Civil Aeronautics Board in addition to the cargo-carrying capacity of the scheduled passenger airlines. Air freight is best considered after the nature of passenger operations has been discussed, since so much of the traffic is carried by the scheduled trunklines. We shall, therefore, postpone any detailed discussion until later.

The pattern of air routes

The total air route mileage in the USA (given in *Table XXVI*) shorter than that for Europe, yet the area of the USA is roughly the same as Greater Europe, or more than twice that of Western Europe. This fact underlines the greatest single difference between the networks of the two areas, i.e. whereas the European network grew up under the jurisdiction of many sovereign states, the US pattern has been regulated in its growth by a single authority. Before studying the network, it is useful to outline the major steps in the growth of the US air routes since the end of World War I.

A strong feature in airline development has been the indirect aid given by the Federal authorities. Unlike the direct subsidy systems of Europe, which often entailed a measure of control of airline policy, the US governmental function has been chiefly a regulating one. If the US airlines have had a 'fairy godmother', then the Post Office is the body that has fulfilled that role, since except in the very early stages, the Post Office has never operated its own transport, but has relied on private operators throughout.

After World War I, the US Post Office initiated the first regular air routes, beginning with the New York–Washington service opened in 1918, using US Army equipment. The first true transcontinental route was the mail service from Chicago to San Francisco opened in 1920. The significance of this early phase, which ended with the Air Mail Act of 1925 (Kelly Act) and the Air Commerce Act of 1926, can hardly be over-estimated. By these Acts, the carriage of mail was transferred to private operators and the real development of the domestic network had begun. The Air Commerce Act established the principle of Federal regulation of operating facilities, safety requirements and licensing.

The support given by mail contracts enabled passenger traffic to be established on a scheduled basis—a development that gained impetus and recognition with the passing of the Watres Act of 1930. By this Act, increased mail payments were made to help operators develop equipment and services suitable for passenger-carrying. The small and numerous operators of this era were the true progenitors of the modern airlines. The depression years, together with government policy, led to a period of consolidation and company integration, during which many of the present airlines were formed. Attempts to integrate both operators and manufacturers of aircraft through Holding Companies were prohibited by the Air Mail Act of 1934. Subsequently, mergers took place only between aircraft operators—i.e. horizontal integration.

The third phase of development succeeded the passing of the Civil Aeronautics Act in 1938. This statute aimed at co-ordinating the economic regulation of the growing industry by the government, under the jurisdiction of a single body. Within this body, the Civil Aeronautics Authority, the Air Safety Board and the Administrator shared the functions of certification of airlines, safety and licensing. By an order of 1940, control and operation of airways were transferred to the Civil Aeronautics Administration of the Department of Commerce, now the Federal Aviation Agency (FAA), while economic regulation and safety requirements, originally controlled by the Civil Aeronautics Authority and the Air Safety Board were transferred to the single authority—the Civil Aeronautics Board (CAB). All proposed scheduled 'common carrier' air routes had now to be certified by the CAB.

Apart from the emergence of the large trunk operators, smaller feeder services, linking points off the main routes, became an important feature in the pattern. Since 1945, the CAB has granted certification to these operators to such an extent that 200 cities are now served solely by feeder routes, while 160 cities connect both trunk and feeder services (*Fig. 11*). At present, therefore, airlines of all sizes may be found. The definition of a trunkline carrier is not an easy one to make. In its report for 1954,[2] the CAB recognized thirty-seven certificated carriers, of which fourteen were trunkline, three all-cargo, two territorial and eighteen local service carriers. The variation in size of the trunkline carriers was considerable: four had an annual output of over 300 million capacity ton miles, while five produced less than 50 million ton-miles. Thus the first four produced over 70% of the total output and the last five only 6%. In 1961 as *Table XLV* shows, twelve

TABLE XLV

CAPACITY TON/MILES PER ANNUM. US TRUNKLINE OPERATORS
1961 (Thousands)

Airline	C.T.M.
United	1,712,136
American	1,370,966
T.W.A.	1,347,846
Eastern	1,220,082
Delta	486,769
Northwest	367,305
National	303,581
Braniff	302,087
Continental	249,020
Western	224,819
Northeast	186,100
Capital	135,127

Source: *CAB Handbook of Airline Statistics 1962*

trunklines dominated the network, the largest producing almost 2,000 million c.t.m.s a year. Together, the group provides some 90% of the total output.

We may now turn to consider the present pattern of routes and the cities they serve. *Table XLV* showed that much of the traffic on the US network is in the hands of the nine biggest airlines. When one looks at the routes themselves, one finds that here, too, relatively few routes account for a high percentage of traffic. A simple route map shows that the country is served by a comprehensive network that covers practically the whole area, but with a marked concentration in the eastern half of the country. To obtain a truer picture *Fig. 10* should be consulted. The density of traffic carried by the network shows enormous variation. Over half the traffic is generated between 100 pairs of cities, while the leading twenty-five pairs alone account for 30%. Note that the availability of passenger origin and destination figures also enables a far more accurate picture of conditions to be constructed than was possible for Europe.

The salient features of the airline network may be briefly analysed. Concentration of traffic is marked in the north-east, on the Pacific coast region and on the trans-continental routes joining east and west. Traffic is low within the area of the High Plains and the Cordillera. Very significant is the density of traffic between Miami and the north-east, particularly through New York and Chicago. In terms of stage length operated, medium- and long-haul routes are important, but many of the sectors are short stage—i.e. less than 500 miles. The closely spaced cities of the north-eastern manufacturing belt offer many stages within the 500-mile limit producing a pattern most nearly analogous to the European case. Short-stage operation is also manifest in the field of feeder-line services, as will be discussed later on.

Trans-continental routes are mainly long and medium haul in character, but aircraft operate not only non-stop transits, e.g. Los Angeles–New York (2,475 miles), which represent long sector distances, but also services that stop at one or more intermediate points. Such operations consist of stage lengths of medium size, e.g. New York–Chicago–Los Angeles includes one stage of 724 miles and a final one of 1,751 miles. The mid-continental cities derive much of their importance in the airline world from their position as 'half-way houses' on the main trans-continental routes. In dealing with trans-continental routes,

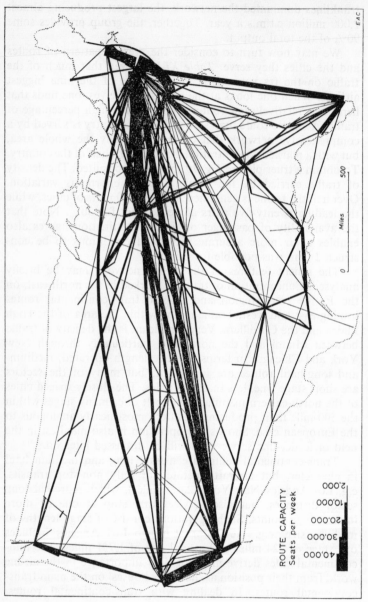

ROUTE CAPACITY
Seats per week

40,000
30,000
20,000
10,000
2,000

Figure 10 Air traffic in the United States (scheduled air services, 1962)

therefore, it must be remembered that passenger origin and destination figures will not give any indication of the number of stages involved, and in fact most trans-continental traffic involves more than one stage. This is in contrast to short stage routes, where each passenger usually travels over only one stage to his destination.

As in Europe, certain stretches of the American domestic network are key sectors in the sense that they carry a significant proportion of through traffic. Outstanding in this field must be counted those sectors that form part of the trans-continental routes. New York–Chicago is perhaps the prime example, for not only does this stretch carry the heavy traffic originating in, or destined for, these two cities, but also traffic bound for destinations on the west coast, particularly Los Angeles, San Francisco and Seattle, and traffic destined for other mid-continental cities.

The Pacific coast concentration is far less marked than the larger network in the east and, unlike the latter, is oriented north–south. The most important sector is that between Los Angeles and San Francisco, followed by San Francisco to Seattle. Whereas surface competition is very real in the east, the more difficult terrain of the Pacific coast states gives greater opportunity for the airlines, even on short sector distances. Some of the smaller feeder-lines operate very short stages, e.g. West Coast Airlines show an average flight stage of only sixty-three miles, while the average passenger trip is 179 miles.

The presence of feeder routes has already been suggested and they form in the aggregate a significant element in the pattern of the whole country. That such a feeder system is necessary in a country of continental size is recognized by the CAB which grants certification to local service operators. Most of these services serve to fill gaps in the trunkline system. *Fig. 11* shows the cities served by trunk- and feeder-line operations and illustrates the relationship between the two. Once again the distinction between east and west is manifest. West of the Mississippi, a few key cities act as junctions between trunk- and feeder-lines, the latter forming a conspicuous element right through to the west coast. The dense pattern of dots near Los Angeles pinpoints the helicopter network of Los Angeles Airways, an ultra-short stage service, and one of the first of its kind in the USA.

In the eastern half of the continent, feeder services are not so obvious. Marked development occurs in areas poorly served

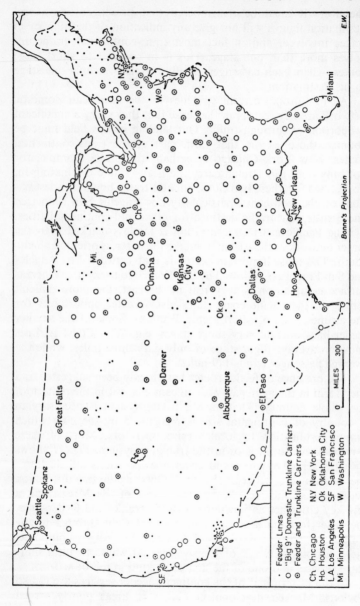

Figure 11 Trunkline and feeder line service points in the United States. Based on figures from *World Airline Record*, 1955

either by trunk connections, or more particularly by circuitous rail connections. The area north of Chicago is a good example. Where train services are poor, e.g. as a result of circuitous routes, air transport benefits. Thus the smaller towns within a 100-mile radius of Milwaukee show apparently anomalous discrepancies in importance. Madison and Muskegon, both within the 100-mile limit, are conspicuous examples, but a study of the rail timetable shows that whereas Madison–Milwaukee is a direct connection involving a mileage of approximately seventy miles, Muskegon–Milwaukee involves a train journey of some 300 miles. The difference between air and rail mileages in the latter case favours the more direct air service. The difference is reflected in fares also : the air fare between Madison and Milwaukee is nearly 50% greater than the rail equivalent, yet the Muskegon rates show the air fare to be less than the rail fare for the journey from Milwaukee. Similar cases may be found to exist between the towns of the north-east and south-east as far as Atlanta. Here again indifferent rail service is evident.

From a general study of the traffic pattern, we may now consider two further aspects of the American network that throw light on its character. The importance of distance has already become manifest in dealing with stage length operated, but we must look at the implications of distance more minutely. Despite the continental proportions of the USA, the average length of a passenger's journey is approximately 550 miles, while some two-thirds of the passengers make journeys of less than 500 miles. *Table XLVI* illustrates the position in more detail, and reveals that distances from 100–300 miles are the most important. It can be seen that such an overall picture as that given in the table masks considerable regional differences. The closely spaced cities of the north-eastern seaboard are a distinct contrast to the mid-continental cities in terms of distance separation, e.g. all the New England towns from Hartford and Springfield to Boston and Providence are less than 150 miles from each other, while Denver's nearest large neighbour is Omaha, some 485 miles distant. In the southern states, also, distances are great between cities. *Table XLVII*, based on CAB findings, shows the regional differences.

In summary, it may be said that although the US network is predominantly a medium- and long-haul system, short stages are by no means unimportant. The majority of passengers make

TABLE XLVI

DISTANCES TRAVELLED BY US AIRLINE PASSENGERS

Distance travelled (miles)	% of passengers carried (Scheduled Services)
0 –99	5·7
100–199	20·4
200–299	18·3
300–399	13·5
400–499	7·5
Over 500	34·6

Source: *Airline Traffic Survey*, Civil Aeronautics Board

TABLE XLVII

DISTANCES TRAVELLED BY US AIRLINE PASSENGERS
BY REGIONS

Region	% of total passengers travelling less than 300 miles	% of total passengers travelling more than 1,500 miles
Pacific Coast	30·0	20·6
Far West	30·1	8·6
Mid-West	41·9	4·6
South-east	39·6	2·5
North-east	52·0	6·1

journeys of less than 300 miles, but there is considerable variation between the major regions of the country.

The second aspect of the air transport pattern that must be considered concerns the relevance of city size and function to air traffic generation. In the previous chapter an attempt was made to relate these elements for Europe and we may now consider the US network from this viewpoint. This task is made easier by the fact that statistics relating to the origin and destination of passengers are available for the USA. The CAA[3] divided the towns of the USA into groups according to the size of their population (1940) and plotted the amount of air traffic each group generated. The results are summarized in *Table XLVIII*.

TABLE XLVIII

CITY SIZE AND PASSENGER AND MAIL TRAFFIC GENERATED

Size group	% of total scheduled passenger traffic 1948	% of total mail traffic 1947
Metropolitan districts:		
250,000 or more	76·9	81·2
50,000–249,999	14·3	11·3
Independent cities:		
25,000–49,999	4·4	2·7
Up to 24,999	4·4	4·8

Source: Civil Aeronautics Administration

As in Europe, the bigger cities generated the highest proportion of the traffic.

In a related study[3] the attempt was made to consider the influence of urban function on the amount of traffic generated. Although 1940 population figures were used, and economic statistics of 1935–40, the results are still interesting. The criterion used here was the influence of occupation, or more especially income levels, of the inhabitants. From an evaluation of occupations as applied to individual cities, four city 'types' were recognized:

(a) Market towns—where wholesale trading was the most important occupation.

(b) Industrial towns—where mining or manufacturing was dominant.

(c) Towns where trade and industry were equally important.

(d) Towns where trade and industry were less important than other occupations—i.e. government, finance or professions.

It was suggested that the purchasing power per head of the population was greater in (a) and (d) than in (b), and that consequently (a) and (d) should be more important as generators of air traffic. The study concluded that, in order of importance, the town groups would rank (a), (d), (c), (b).

More recently, E. J. Taaffe[6] has considered the problem of urban size and function in relation to air transport. Using the passenger origin and destination figures for the cities served by regular air services, he calculated a 'passenger index'. This index was determined by first taking sample cities and calculating the number of air passengers per 1,000 population and obtaining a median index. When this index was applied to the cities under review, certain of them were found to generate more or less than the median. In the north-east, some cities had an index below what their size would suggest. Traffic shadow here plays an important part. New York, in particular, casts a general shadow over the surrounding city clusters. Boston, with an index greater than the median, lies beyond the immediate influence of New York, but Philadelphia and Baltimore both appear overshadowed by New York and Washington. Other noticeable shadows appear between Cleveland and Pittsburgh, in southern Michigan and among the smaller cities near Chicago. The index figures showed[6] that some of the greatest traffic generators are not among the biggest cities. Washington and resorts like Miami and Phoenix are examples, while regional centres beyond the environs of the north-east likewise show high indices, e.g. Denver, Dallas and Atlanta.

Dealing with the matter at greater length, Taaffe notes that the 106 largest traffic generators account for 90% of the total traffic. Of these cities, 81% of those with an urban population greater than 500,000 have a high passenger index, while only 14% of the cities with a population of less than 125,000 show a high index. The traffic flow is, then, predominantly between the larger urban conglomerations.

Traffic shadow is most marked in the north-east, as already seen. Elsewhere, the difference between medium and high index figures among the towns of the south-east picks out the regional centres. In particular, Charlotte and Atlanta are outstanding. Poor rail connections between the north and the south-east tend to help air transport, and the number of low index cities in the south-east is less than might be expected. The wider spread of cities in the western half of the continent reduces the influence of traffic shadow, e.g. Texas shows widely scattered medium index cities, notably Dallas, Houston, El Paso, Midland and Amarillo. Fort Worth seems to be struggling under the shadow of Dallas. The area of traffic shadow extending from a major city is variable, as Taaffe suggests. In the eastern half of the country, he takes a 120-mile radius as the basis and his figures show that a low *per capita* generation of air traffic does exist among smaller cities within 120 miles of a larger city. Outside the eastern half of the country, the radius of influence appears greater, e.g. San Antonio, although more than 120 miles from Dallas and Houston, appears to be within their shadow.

When traffic shadow has been considered, residual differences between size and traffic generation, as indicated by the passenger index, must be due to other causes. Taaffe then considers the non-shadow cities in terms of function. It is interesting to compare his findings with those of the CAA study referred to earlier, and to the results obtained in our European study. He groups the passenger generating ability of city types as follows:

Greatest generation of traffic : (*a*) Resorts and special function cities.
(*b*) Wholesale and retail markets.
(*c*) Diversified cities.
Least generation of traffic : (*d*) Manufacturing and mining.

Examples : (*a*) Reno, San Diego, Las Vegas, Washington, Jacksonville, Tampa and Miami.
(*b*) El Paso, Boise, Salt Lake City, Denver, Omaha, Wichita, Dallas and Jackson.
(*c*) Portland, Spokane, Minneapolis, Des Moines, Kansas City and Charlotte.
(*d*) New Orleans, Cincinnati, Knoxville, Duluth, Norfolk, Scranton, Grand Rapids (Michigan), Detroit and Peoria.

The length of haul also contributes to index differences, particularly beyond the orbit of the north-east, where higher indices are common. The presence of special function cities and the diffuse urban pattern contribute, but distance is important and most cities outside the north-east are concerned with long- or medium-haul traffic. An important aspect concerns the relation between the air route and surface alternatives. In this respect, the dominance of New York and Chicago is relevant. The size of these centres is so great that although overnight train services connect them, airlines still generate an enormous traffic. The dominance of these two cities extends most acutely to the distance passengers may travel from them by overnight rail services. Within this radius, surface transport appears to be most competitive with air transport. Beyond it, travel enters the medium- and long-haul category and air transport benefits accordingly. The differences between the passenger indices of cities within the overnight radius and those beyond it is perceptible. Within the orbit of Chicago and New York (in theory) lie many of the southern towns, but in practice no overnight rail service is operated except to Atlanta. Elsewhere, arrival times in the southern cities are inconvenient. Outside their orbit, important air transport 'zones' occur in the Far West and Pacific coast, in Texas and Florida. Poor surface connections north of Chicago, and in parts of the south-east, contribute to higher air transport passenger indices.

In his conclusion, Taaffe suggests that the two most important factors affecting the development of US passenger air traffic are, firstly, the size of the urban population and, secondly, its distribution. In addition, city function and the availability of good surface transport must be considered as other factors.

Air freight

The carriage of cargo by air is essentially a post-war development. Before 1941 most traffic of this kind travelled by 'air express', i.e. small packages sent as quickly as possible on passenger services. The war itself gave ample opportunity for experience in this field of air transport, with the result that true freight traffic has made enormous strides since 1945 (*Table XLIX*). As the table shows, the air freight ton mileage has increased enormously between 1946 and 1961, and, since 1959, at a rate greater than that experienced in passenger and mail traffic. Great as this increase has been, it represents only a minute proportion of the ton/mileage worked each year by surface transport (*see Table L*). Another point of interest brought out by *Table XLIX* is the relationship between all-freight carriers and the regular trunklines. All-freight companies are essentially a post-war phenomenon, operating in the early stages by contract. By a decision of the CAB in 1949, four carriers were granted certificates for regular operation— two trans-continental, one north–south and one local service operator in Texas. In 1964, the CAB listed three all-freight carriers. In the immediate post-war era, the domestic trunkline companies were preoccupied with re-equipment and re-organization, with the result that the all-freight operators carried the bulk of the freight traffic, but since 1948 the trunklines have

TABLE XLIX

AIR FREIGHT IN THE USA

Ton/Miles (Thousands)

Year	Domestic Trunk carriers	All-freight carriers
1946	38,085	—
1949	121,519	11,666
1952	157,658	86,447
1955	223,829	102,299
1958	286,919	208,584
1961	441,206	259,519

Source: *CAB Handbook of Airline Statistics*

TABLE L

PERCENTAGE OF TOTAL TON/MILES OPERATED BY
TYPES OF TRANSPORT IN THE USA
1961

	%
Railway	43·9
Highway	22·9
Inland Waterways	15·7
Pipelines	17·5
Airways	0·07

Source: *Statistical Abstract of the United States*

played an increasingly important part in freight operations. At present the situation is unstable and we may not expect a stabilization for some considerable time. With this in mind, we may consider, finally, the opportunities and characteristics of the freight market.

Taking freight haulage as a whole, the chief geographical characteristic is the predominance of east–west or 'cross-grain' traffic. The industrial north-east acts as the focus of the country, into which pour the raw materials of industry and the agricultural products of the mid-continent. North–south traffic is marked along the Atlantic coast, the Mississippi and between the mid-continental cities, from Omaha, Kansas City, and Dallas to Houston in Texas.

The leading commodities concerned in these great traffic movements are low value, bulky goods, of which coal, industrial raw materials and agricultural produce are the chief. Petroleum movements from the south-west oilfields by pipeline and tanker to the north-east represent another bulk movement. From the north-east flow the complementary cargoes of finished goods, generally of higher unit value and lower unit weight. General freight traffic into the north-east is, therefore, two to three times heavier than the complementary westward and southward traffic. Other major elements in the overall pattern result from the location of the USA's chief timber resources in the Pacific Northwest and in the South, and the specialized commodity movements, represented by off-season fruit and vegetable products, which often span the continent. Finally, ubiquitous products of a bulky nature, e.g. sand, bricks, give rise to heavy local movements within individual state boundaries.

Against this broad pattern we must consider the market for the air freighter. It becomes obvious at once that the bulk of the total freight traffic of the USA is entirely unsuited to air transport; coal and iron ore are unlikely to fly for many years yet. Of the major traffic streams, only the westward movement of manu-factured goods from the north-east appears at all possible as a source of revenue. Many finished products from this area fulfil the requirements of air cargo—particularly those of low bulk and high value. The present pattern of air-freight movements reveals the growing importance of this trade route to the operator. In 1948[3] the Middle Atlantic and East North Central regions des-patched three-fifths of all goods sent by air: the carriage of these goods from the north-east to the western and southern markets involves movement along already established passenger trunk-lines. The chief difficulty for the air-freight carrier on these routes is the unbalanced flow of traffic, for most of the goods are westbound. Eastbound traffic, as we have already hinted, is likely to be small, since most of the commodities are bulky raw materials or food products. One immediate possibility is the tapping of the early fruit and vegetable traffic from the truck regions of California and the Pacific Northwest. North–south movement is again unbalanced, the bulk of the available traffic being southbound.

In conclusion, it may be suggested that considerable potential exists for the air freighter, not only on established trans-continental routes, but between areas not served by such lines. The development of a closer pattern of inter-regional traffic seems eminently possible and is a field that may well prove to be economic for the all-freight carrier. With the continued growth of industrial areas outside the north-east, e.g. in Texas and California, a more balanced traffic movement may be possible. (*See Table XIII* for commodities carried.)

Airline shape and layout

It may be remembered that the chief characteristic of European airlines is the radial pattern of their routes. The presence of numerous sovereign states that regulate their services through the medium of bilateral agreements, together with the short stages operated, results in a radiation of routes from the capital cities. The greater size of the USA in comparison with Western Europe, and the fact that a single political authority is involved, would suggest that a far greater variety of airline layouts would result. That this is so may easily be determined from a study of sample cases. All the main types of pattern are represented from the linear to the circular. The tendency for a particular network to assume a certain shape will depend upon the size and position of the cities it serves, the category of its operations— whether trunkline or local—and the presence of limiting factors such as political restrictions on routes operated (either internally, or as the result of bilateral agreements with other countries). Most airlines conform to one or other of four patterns, i.e. radial, circular, grid or linear. Variations are common, e.g. a linear pattern may consist of two major routes running in parallel, forming a 'parallel' pattern. The study of airlines from this point of view is a neglected aspect of the subject, but one which can throw much light on the suitability of the individual network in relation to rail and road communications and the broader pattern represented by the cities served. In unpublished work,[1] W. S. Barry has considered the layout of four US airlines and his results are of interest to the airline operator as well as to the geographer.

We can outline only a few examples to illustrate the major

relationships. Trunklines, which by definition connect major cities in widely dispersed regions, are usually linear in layout. American Airlines, with important routes connecting eastern and western America, are an example of this among the trans-continental operators. Smaller trunklines, especially when they

TABLE LI

THE DEVELOPMENT OF US SCHEDULED DOMESTIC AIRLINES

Year	No. of air-lines	Revenue ton/miles (million)	%Revenue ton/mile load factor	%Revenue Passenger/ mile load factor	Average speed (m.p.h.)	Revenue Passenger/ miles flown	
						1st Class %	Air Coach %
1926	13	—	—	—	—	—	—
1930	43	8	—	—	—	—	—
1933	25	17	—	39·4	116	—	—
1936	24	45	—	54·5	149	—	—
1939	18	80	47·3	56·2	153	—	—
1942	19	177	65·7	72·2	159	—	—
1945	20	428	82·0	88·1	153	—	—
1948	31	717	52·0	58·0	176	—	—
1951	36	1,233	61·0	69·6	192	88	12
1954	31	1,903	56·1	63·4	222	68	32
1961	43	3,583	47·7	55·4	—	45	55

Sources: *World Airline Record*, 1955
CAB Handbook of Airline Statistics

serve a more compact area of limited extension, assume a radial or grid pattern. Stage lengths are often shorter and development is intensive rather than extensive. The grid-like network of Eastern Air Lines is a case in point. In an intermediate position among the trunklines may be considered the essentially parallel shape of National Airlines, whose linear shape consists of a westerly route from New York to Washington, Jacksonville, Tampa and Miami and an easterly component from Washington and New York to Miami directly.

Smaller operators show a profusion of shapes. The short stage lengths and evenly scattered townships of southern New England result in the close radial pattern of Northeast Airlines based on Boston and New York. Continental Air Lines, covering the growing towns of Texas and Oklahoma, is another example of a radial layout. The narrow zone of occupation along the Pacific west coast gives a marked linear pattern to Southwest Airways, whose network runs from Los Angeles northwards to Crescent City, California and Medford, Oregon.

Comparison between the air layout of routes and the local rail pattern brings out sharply the relation between air mileage and its railway equivalent. Differences may often be referred to topographical peculiarities which are very relevant in many parts of the United States. Broader studies relating layout of airlines to the resource patterns of the region, or regions, served may also be commended. The author can do no more than suggest that the interested reader pursue the matter in more detail for himself.

REFERENCES

1. Barry, W. S. *Air Transport in the U.S.A.: a study in the Economic Geography of the growth and function of selected Airlines*, Ph.D. Thesis, London, 1954. (Unpublished.)
2. Civil Aeronautics Board. Annual Reports. (Washington, D.C.)
3. Civil Aeronautics Administration. *Inter-City Airline Passenger Traffic Pattern*, 1950.
   Civil Aeronautics Administration. *Office of Airports, Economic Character of Communities*, 1948.
   Civil Aeronautics Administration. *Enplaned Traffic by Communities*, 1948.
4. Hartshorne, R. 'A New Map of the Manufacturing Belt of North America', *Economic Georgraphy*, Volume 12, 1936.
5. Klan, Spencer. 'Twelve Thousand Company Planes', *Fortune*, January 1956.
6. Taaffe, E. J. 'Air Transportation and US Urban Distribution', *Geographical Review*, Volume 46, 1956.
7. Caves, R. E. *Air Transport and its regulators*. Harvard, 1962.

AIR TRANSPORT IN UNDER-DEVELOPED AREAS

Our attention so far as been focused on the industrialized economies of Western Europe and the USA and we must now turn to consider air transport under different conditions. If we use Europe or the USA as a yardstick, then it must be admitted that a large proportion of the globe comes under the heading of 'under-developed' (*Fig. 7*). We are confronted with an enormous range of physical and economic conditions, as far apart as the cold of the Canadian northlands and the heat of the tropical selva of the Amazon basin. Surface accessibility varies widely; in many areas, human and animal transport still play an important role. Population density may vary from the sparsity of Siberia and northern Canada to the dense groupings of south-east Asia. In short, the term 'under-developed' covers a host of situations.

Common to all is a lack of modern transport facilities. Even though the demand may be there, it is not effective, usually through a lack of capital resources, but sometimes because of rigorous physical conditions. Transport is essential to the development of a country, for without it real specialization is impossible. In geographical terms, therefore, all under-developed countries are areas where regional specialization has hardly begun.

Two chief sets of factors are involved in this lack of transport, which may be found separately, or more usually together:

(*a*) Physical difficulties resulting from relief, climate or vegetation regimes.

(*b*) Economic difficulties resulting from under- or over-population, lack of capital resources and low *per capita* incomes.

On this basis we may recognize three categories of under-developed territories:

(*i*) Low population density and high national and *per capita* incomes, e.g. Canada.

(*ii*) Low population density and low national and *per capita* incomes, e.g. some of the African states, Central American Republics.

(*iii*) High population density and low national and *per capita* incomes, e.g. India, Indonesia, China.

Difficult physical regimes may apply to any of these categories. The greatest advances at the present moment are usually to be found among the countries under category (*i*) and it is to these countries that one must turn in order to see how aviation fits into the picture. Development is more variable within the remaining two categories.

Finally, we must view the preceding background against the results of our studies of Europe and the USA, which suggested above all that air transport flourished most in highly industrialized communities where the urban population was most marked. Passenger traffic formed the chief source of revenue in these instances. If these results are valid, one might well ask—how can air transport be important in under-developed areas where none of these conditions is fulfilled? That it can be important in these areas implies a different role, or at least a change of emphasis.

The chief transport need for an under-developed country is for bulk movement of raw materials, agricultural produce and manufactured goods (that have either been imported or produced on the spot). When this provision has been made, aviation takes its place as the long-range mobile arm of industry, commerce and, eventually, tourism, much as in Europe or the USA. We are here concerned with the phases of development leading up to this position.

In the early or 'pioneer' phase, the question arises—what are the resources of the area? Are they big enough to make expensive road and rail projects worthwhile? The more difficult the terrain involved, the more vital it is that an accurate assessment be made. The aeroplane provides one way of answering these questions and its role at this early stage includes topographical and mineral surveys and the establishment of the first camps and bases. This may then be succeeded by a phase when aircraft provide the major transport services. The machines used must be adapted to difficult conditions, be simple to maintain and able to operate out of improvised strips with the minimum of radio or other ground aids. Except, perhaps, for the main base, the large airport is unlikely to figure prominently in the network of routes, and large passenger aircraft give way to smaller and more ubiquitous machines like the De Havilland (Canada) 'Beaver' and 'Otter', and the helicopter. As progress continues, the larger DC–3 and more recent freighters may be employed. Such seem to be the trends one may see in the development of territories like northern Canada or Australia. We may, indeed, perceive the outlines of a number of definite phases, i.e. :

(a) Pioneer phase : Use of aircraft for surveys of all kinds, e.g. topographical, forest or mineral surveys.
   If development of the resources seems justified, aircraft are used to establish the first camps and to aid in the construction of surface links.
(b) Establishment of primary road or rail routes. Beginning of exploitation on a large scale. Aircraft still play a vital role as both passenger and freighter machines.
(c) Final phase : Growth of industry and settlement may follow if conditions are suitable. Air transport assumes a more 'normal' role, deriving most of its revenue from passenger, mail and specialized freight operations.

This plan is particularly applicable to countries we have classified as category (i), for here we are dealing with almost uninhabited areas adjacent to more populous zones enjoying a high standard of living. The key to the situation is normally difficult physical conditions, particularly climatic ones. Indeed, as we shall see, conditions may be such that development may never proceed to stage (c) outlined above.

Countries that come under the remaining two categories present a variety of possibilities, and in some instances the area to be developed may already be settled, sometimes densely, e.g.

Indonesia. The 'pioneer phase' in such places may take on a somewhat different plan, but the transport situation is essentially similar. Aircraft adapted to operation from improvised strips and without extensive aids are again required, and since many tropical countries are involved, the chief hazards lie in weather conditions and jungle-clad terrain. Once again aircraft may be used to speed the establishment of surface routes that are essential for large-scale development.

We may now turn to consider an example. Since, from the very nature of the present situation, development is incomplete, we may sketch out the bold outlines and consider individual projects only in more detail. For the reader who wishes to extend this fascinating study, further examples may be considered by consulting the books and papers listed in the bibliography. Here we shall consider development in northern Canada, one of the most striking examples of modern pioneering.

Northern Canada (*Arctic and sub-Arctic zones*)

Activity in Canada's 'outback' had its origins in the early activities of the English companies, like the Hudson's Bay Company, in the eighteenth and nineteenth centuries, but the modern era of development has its roots in the inter-war years (1918–39) with the operations of the bush pilots. Both the older fur trade and the newer mining activities near Lake Athabasca and Great Slave Lake were largely dependent upon this hardy breed for their maintenance in the field. Sporadic though these operations often were, much experience of cold weather operations was built up, and proved invaluable to the vastly greater activity during the war and since. The spectacular developments of the post-war period in this vast territory have captured the popular imagination and much has been written about them. Progress has been aided by the fact that within the political boundaries of Canada one finds not only undeveloped ground, but also a ribbon of denser population and economic development. From the St. Lawrence lowlands and the Ontario peninsula in the east to the wedge-shaped band of the settled prairies and the communities of the west coast, lies a thread of human occupation dependent on agriculture and industry and enjoying a high standard of living. In aviation, no less than in other fields, this is an important fact, for not only are capital resources available, but an industry that is already familiar with many of the problems

of the adjacent unsettled hinterland. From the days of the old
Fokker 'Universal' and Bellanca monoplanes to the present
generation of aircraft, the Canadian aircraft industry has always
been in the forefront where the operation of aircraft in cold
climates and difficult terrains is concerned.

The geographical background

The term 'Northern Canada' is used here to denote the Arctic
and sub-Arctic zones, whose delineation is based on climate.[4]
Fig. 12 shows the southern limits of the area thus defined. The
sheer size of the region is staggering—approximately 2,700,000
square miles—and the distances with which men are faced are
continental in span. Hudson Bay divides the territory into two
unequal parts, the smaller eastern segment converging on the
settled St. Lawrence valley and the Ontario peninsula, and the
western segment adjoining the prairies and west-coast settlements.
Over the whole region, population density is less than five persons
per square mile.

No discussion of Northern Canada can be contemplated
without consideration of its physical geography and we must
consider transport problems in the light of the challenge it
represents. The whole area may be divided into three main
regions (*Fig. 12*), of which the Canadian Shield forms by far
the largest. Westwards the Shield is succeeded by the narrow
extension of the Great Plains and finally by the folded rocks
of the Western Cordillera.

The Shield, built up of igneous and metamorphic rocks of
Pre-Cambrian age, represents the core of the whole continent.
It is an area of subdued relief except for its upturned eastern
and south-eastern margin. The mountains of Ungava province,
and the steep mountain edge flanking the north shore of the
St. Lawrence, represent the only sections of high relief. The
central region of the Shield has been depressed and is now partly
occupied by the waters of Hudson Bay. By far the greatest
difficulties facing surface movement arise from the modifications
made by the glaciations of the Pleistocene period. The scraping
action of the ice sheets has left much bare rock, hummocky in
appearance and covered with a fine network of lakes and swamps.
From the coniferous forests of the south, vegetation thins out
near the transition from sub-Arctic to Arctic into the tundra,
dominated for the most part by mosses, heaths, lichens and

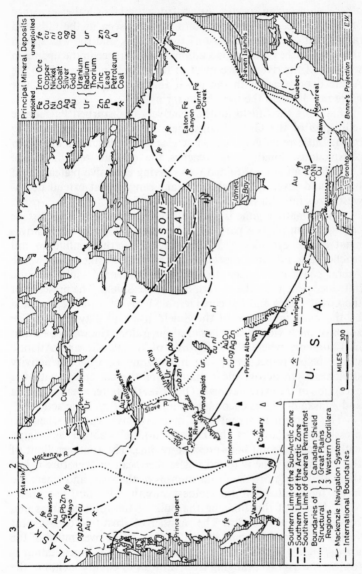

Figure 12 Location and resources map of Canada

other low-growing species. Apart from the lakes, other evidence
of the disturbed drainage pattern is to be seen in the falls and
rapids that characterize most of the streams, and the widespread
areas of marsh. Flooding is a common occurrence in the upstream
sections of the rivers since most of them drain northwards to the
Arctic depression, with the result that the upper reaches thaw
more rapidly than the mouths in spring.

Flanking the Shield lie the relatively undisturbed Palaeozoic
sediments of the Great Plains, here reduced to a very narrow
band. Little relief is evident, but glacial modifications are again
conspicuous. Finally, one reaches the difficult terrain of the
Cordillera, an area of folded rocks giving extensive plateaux and
basins and several distinct mountain ranges, that extend north-
westwards into Alaska.

The climatic regime is vital to aviation, and here also surface
configuration plays a part. The Cordillera lies astride the movement of the cyclones of Pacific origin, but their influence still
reaches the interior, especially in winter. Further, the whole
Arctic coastline is open to northern influence, while Atlantic
influence penetrates the eastern half of the Shield. The presence of
the Great Lakes and the considerable body of water represented
by the numerous lakes of the Shield itself all play a part. The
zones of most violent weather are found along the west coast and
in Labrador, where the full force of the Pacific and Atlantic
storm belts, respectively, is felt. A zone of cyclonic activity
stretches right across the remainder of the continent, with the
exception of the extreme north. Only over this latter area in Canada
and Alaska does one encounter a minimum of cyclonic activity.

This pattern is accentuated in the winter season, when depressions may disrupt the calmer 'prairie' weather associated
with the continental high-pressure regime. The southern limit of
the sub-Arctic zone is found where the mean temperature is less
than 50°F. for more than four months of the year, and where the
mean temperature of the coldest month does not rise above
32°F. North of this limit lie the bulk of the forested areas and
beyond them the tundra. The number of frost-free days a year
varies with location from 50 to 100 days, while over much of the
area (*Fig. 12*) the subsoil is permanently frozen. Precipitation is
low on the average, ranging from a mean of twenty inches in the
south to less than five inches in the north. Much of it falls as snow,
especially in the autumn. Exceptions occur in the littoral zones—

e.g. parts of the Labrador coast receive more than 200 inches of rainfall per annum. Visibility varies widely—a period of calm weather with good visibility may be rapidly succeeded by storms in which wind-driven snow may reduce surface visibility to ten yards. These cold conditions close rivers and coastal seas to navigation for up to seven months of the year and it is only in late summer and early autumn that full navigation may be feasible.

What are the main effects of this climate upon various transport forms? Water navigation must, obviously, be severely restricted, not only by the winter freeze, but by flooding in the spring thaw. In addition, the numerous rapids in the stream beds constitute barriers, as a study of any individual case proves, e.g. on the Mackenzie River system, the Athabasca River has an upper steamer limit at the junction of the McLeod River. From there the river is navigable, despite minor rapids, for 325 miles as far as Grand Rapids. Here a fall of sixty feet in half a mile prohibits navigation. From Grand Rapids, rapids continually interrupt navigation as far as Fort McMurray. Below this, the river remains navigable as far as its mouth on Lake Athabasca. Other streams and the Mackenzie itself reveal a similar state of affairs.

Apart from the more easily recognized difficulties, road and rail transport suffer from the influence of frost-heaving in winter. The effect of this process—a characteristic one—is to raise up portions of the ballast and track until it looks as if an earthquake had affected the line. Unless precautions are taken, road metal may be cracked and broken by frost action. In any case, operations are restricted in most cases to the summer season, which may mean only three-four months. Not the least of the worries concerns the supply of fuel, which may be rendered difficult over the greater part of the Shield.

Air transport scores heavily from the fact that it needs no track. The construction of airfields, although expensive, is by no means impossible and the problems are not as acute as those found when the vehicle requires a track.* Apart from major bases, aircraft can be operated from small strips or from the lakes, where necessary. The variable weather conditions, and particularly cold weather, pose the greatest problems. Weight must be sacrificed in order to protect the machine, its crew and cargo from the effects of the cold. Ground protection is often

* Note the development of surface vehicles of the caterpillar-track type such as the 'Snocat'.

needed for the aircraft when starting up, in order to get the engines running at their working temperatures as quickly as possible. In view of the widely scattered radio aids and alternative landing grounds, larger fuel reserves are necessary in case of diversion through bad weather. Icing conditions are more frequently found near coastal regions than in the drier interior, where the temperature is often below the critical range in any case. The proximity of the magnetic pole in the more northerly regions makes the magnetic compass almost useless, but the establishment of new radar aids and the use of directional gyros, whose rate of precession may be allowed for, has gone far to overcome this particular difficulty. Forced descents are fortunately a remote possibility, but provision must be made in the form of emergency kits and clothing in case of such mishaps. In addition, rescue aircraft are kept ready at the more important bases.

The resources of the area, which alone make development worth while, may now be discussed. By far the most valuable are the vast mineral reserves that are to be found in the Shield, Great Plains and the Cordillera. Although much of the area is still being surveyed, the known deposits have proved valuable enough to warrant exploitation. In the Shield, the igneous and metamorphic rocks represent one of the greatest mineral reserves in the world. Most significant are the sources of radio-active material—uranium, thorium and radium—but silver, lead and zinc, copper, nickel, cobalt and gold are also present (*Fig. 12*). In Quebec and Labrador lie the iron ores of the Burnt Creek region, with possibly greater resources further north near Ungava Bay.

The Great Plains are potentially a source of petroleum and include the vast reserves of the Athabasca tar sands, which so far have not proved worthy of exploitation. The wartime Canoil project and the isolated station at Norman Wells suggest the possibilities in the region. Within the Cordilleran province, coal is known in Upper Athabasca, while gold, silver, lead and zinc are known and worked. Hydro-electric potential is another asset, while the forested zones of northern British Columbia, Yukon and the Mackenzie are estimated to contain 100,000 million board feet of timber, as yet unused.

Lastly, the position of Northern Canada in present-day global strategy has encouraged the setting up of bases and warning radar systems, all of which contribute indirectly to the possibilities of resource development.

Air transport and development in Northern Canada

Aircraft were first used in the 1920's, when trappers and pro-spectors chartered aircraft to carry themselves and their equip-ment into the sparsely populated regions north of Edmonton. The network of 'bush' routes that came into being was centred on a number of strategically placed bases, e.g. Edmonton and Whitehorse. Most of the traffic hauled by these pioneers was freight. Mining machinery, like diamond drills weighing about 1,800 lb., explosives, food supplies and similar cargo were taken into the newly discovered sites that sprang up from Dawson and Aklavik in the north to Lake Athabasca and southern Hudson Bay in the south. By 1934 freight costs averaged $2·24 per ton/mile, while passenger rates averaged about $20 per head for 100 miles. Whereas the aircraft were capable of carrying up to a ton of freight, costs restricted development to the most profitable resources. On return journeys, the machines brought out the ore samples or furs that their customers produced. When mining development proved economic, tractor trains were used to haul bulk cargoes in the winter months. Nevertheless, the aeroplane still remained the key to the whole scheme.

Much experience was obtained of cold weather flying as a result of these activities. The aircraft used were small and rugged, and capable of operating from land, water or snow. At first, imported machines like the Fokker 'Universal' were employed, but the growing Canadian aircraft industry began modifying, and later producing, designs adapted to the conditions. Perhaps the most famous was the Noorduyn 'Norseman' from which the present-day 'Beaver' and 'Otter' aircraft have been developed. The Norseman, a single-engined, high-wing monoplane, could be operated on wheels, floats or ski, and was capable of carrying up to eight passengers, or 2,000 lb. of freight. Easily removed seats enabled any combination of load to be carried up to the permitted gross weight of the machine (7,400 lb.). It proved simple to operate and maintain, yet had a small field performance that matched the terrain it operated from. *Table LII* gives the leading performance figures for this machine, which set the fashion for many modern derivatives.

The navigation facilities of the pre-war era were negligible, and although radio communication between bases was available, most of the actual flying was by contact navigation. The modern operator owes much to the pilots concerned, men like W. May

TABLE LII

PERFORMANCE CHARACTERISTICS OF THE NOORDUYN
'NORSEMAN' MK. V

Version	Cruising speed 75% power (m.p.h.)	Climb to 5,000 ft. Full load (mins.)	Landing speed (m.p.h.)	Cruising range with full load 75% power (statute miles)
Landplane	148	6·5	68	1,150
Seaplane	130	—	68	—
Skiplane	142	—	68	—

Source: *Jane's All the World's Aircraft*, 1946

of Canadian Airways Ltd., Berry of the same company and
McMillan of Mackenzie Air Services Ltd.

By 1939 the outline of the present network could be discerned.
Services connected the major northern bases—Whitehorse, Dawson and Mayo—while others from these points, or from Edmonton
and Winnipeg, served the mines of Port Radium, Yellowknife
and the Mackenzie Basin in the west, and the similar sites near
Flinflon in Manitoba. With the exception of the last, no railroad
or permanent road served these areas. Apart from canoes or
dog teams, only the restricted use of tractor-drawn sleds was
possible.

From this inter-war development has come the much greater
progress of the wartime and post-war years. Wartime progress
was mainly technical—the growth of radio aids and the design
of superior aircraft. The ferry service from Canada through
Alaska to the USSR, although a military project, provided
experience and—more concretely—airfields, that have significance
to civil progress. The strategic vulnerability of Canada's northern
border that resulted from the post-war generation of aircraft
has stimulated survey and the establishment of radar chains and
bases, all of which help the economic exploitation of the area.
Indeed, we may now perceive more clearly the pattern of development that is taking place, and the part aircraft are playing in the
mosaic.

The first point to notice is the relationship of the settled areas
to the pioneer zones. The bulk of the latter lie beyond the reach

of any single group of cities, so that development has advanced from a number of distinct foci stretching right across the continent (*Fig. 13*). East of Hudson Bay, the old-established cities of the St. Lawrence valley act as the business centres, particularly Montreal. The distance of Montreal or Quebec from the mining sites is often too great for direct air contact. Working bases have assumed importance and towns like Seven Islands and Mt. Joli have expanded into a prominence that few would have predicted 100 years ago. West of Hudson Bay the three prairie cities of Winnipeg, Prince Albert and Edmonton act as the foci. From them the northern routes connect with the established transcontinental airways (*Fig. 13*). Edmonton is most strategically placed for contact with the north-west, yet even so it is over 600 miles from Yellowknife, 950 miles from Whitehorse and about 1,500 from Aklavik at the mouth of the Mackenzie. Intermediate bases, established in the formative years before 1939, have become important, e.g. Grande Prairie, Whitehorse and Hay River. Ground communications have been established to some of these points—Grande Prairie is connected to Edmonton by rail, Whitehorse is only connected by rail to Skagway, Alaska, on the coast, but lies on the Alcan Highway, while Hay River is connected southwards by the new Mackenzie Highway and northwards by water navigation. In 1964, the railway to Hay River was completed, and work was in progress on the 55-mile branch to Pine Point.

From these nodal points the air route pattern takes its shape, as may be seen from the map (*Fig. 13*). Since most of the active mining areas have poor surface links, the pattern of development is still in an early pioneer category and freight looms large in proportion to the rest of air traffic. The cost of air freight on the Mackenzie routes averages eighty cents per ton/mile—four times the rate in the USA. Although rail and water will prove costly to extend and freight rates will be correspondingly higher, the figure estimated—six cents per ton/mile—is still a contrast with the air equivalent. We must emphasize the point that no large-scale development can take place without bulk surface carriers. Exploitation by air alone, or with a poor surface link, is a costly business and only the most profitable resources have so far been touched. Of these, the radio-active minerals are the modern equivalent of the earlier attractions of gold in the nineteenth century.

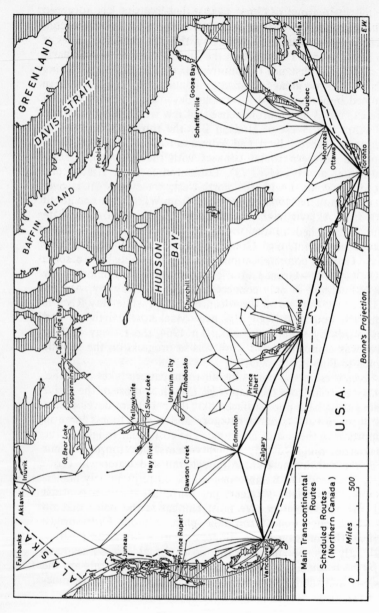

Figure 13 Air routes in Northern Canada, 1964. Based on figures from the *Report of the Public Finance and Transportation Division, Dominion Bureau of Statistics,* and *A.B.C. World Airline Guide*

The intense activity near Lake Athabasca that has succeeded the discovery of the uranium resources in 1947 is a good example. Survey was carried out almost entirely by air and is still going on. By 1951 ore reserve estimates were held to justify a production of 500 tons per day. The initial discoveries at the Ace field near Beaverlodge Lake were followed by further discoveries in the same area. The mine at Ace field was completed in eighteen months[3] between July 1951 and January 1953, and the construction of a service building and a 500-ton capacity ore concentrator followed. Beaverlodge lies 500 miles north of Edmonton by air and 300 miles from the railhead at Waterways. Air transport was used to establish the initial camps and has since gone far to speed up the establishment of the water–rail link needed to carry out the concentrates. Thus, in order to maintain the construction schedule in 1952, some 2,400 tons of building supplies were flown in before the opening of the river navigation season. Aircraft played an important part in the initial building of Uranium City some seven miles from the mine. Here it is intended to house the married employees of all the mines that may eventually be set up in the area. With the establishment of ore production, air transport has become a regular service for both passengers and freight. Saskair operates three round trips a week to Uranium City. In addition, this operator leases equipment for forest fire control and air ambulance services. In a recent year, the company's total revenue was derived from the following sources: mining 40%, government contracts 25%, trapping 20%, fishing 10% and 50% from sportsmen. *Table LIII* gives further details of the company's work in recent years, and serves to illustrate the balance of activity of airlines* covering this region.

The development of the Quebec–Labrador iron ore concessions makes an interesting comparison with the foregoing case. From the very beginning of exploration in 1936 in this almost uninhabited area aircraft have proved indispensable. In 1948 air freighters began the task of transporting material for the construction of the base camp at Burnt Creek on the orefield, ten miles west of the airstrip at Knob Lake (*Figs. 12* and *13*), and 300 miles inland from the St. Lawrence valley at Seven Islands. The primary need was for the construction of a railway between the orefield and Seven Islands, for no navigation

* The other scheduled operator is Canadian Pacific Airlines

TABLE LIII

OPERATING STATISTICS OF SASKAIR

Year	Aircraft fleet	Passengers carried	Freight carried (million lb.)	Mail carried (thou. lb.)	Unduplicated route mileage (approx. miles)
1952	23	6,769	3·2	63·4	
1953	23	12,304	3·8	63·5	
1961	20	18,293	6·1	105·8	1,300
1963	19	11,733	3·7	101·0	

Source: *World Airline Record*, Saskatchewan House, London

was possible on the rivers and no other form of surface link existed.

The whole pattern of growth was unlike that of any other pioneer project. Aircraft supplied material for the construction of the railway not only at Burnt Creek, but at intermediate points between Burnt Creek and Seven Islands. The railway was built from four main points simultaneously, cutting construction time by a half. This 'nodular' progression was a marked contrast from the usual outward movement of rail construction from a single base camp.

The variety of goods that had to be transported may well be imagined when one realizes that until the railway was completed in 1954 all men, provisions and equipment had to go by air. Intensity of operation was the key to the whole project—a lesson learnt from wartime experience and the Berlin Air Lift. During the short summer season when air traffic was possible, a continuous day and night shuttle service was maintained. Some idea of the scale of the project may be appreciated by noting that in the four summer months of 1951, 14,000,000 lb. of equipment and supplies were shifted.[2] Only one specialized freighter—a Fairchild 'Packet' lent by the US Air Force—was in operation in that period, and this machine moved 800 tons of heavy machinery in the two months of June and July. Included within this total were tractors, graders, scrapers and motor vehicles.

The airstrip at the intermediate point of Wacouna was built in ten days in October 1950,[1] despite the onset of fog and intermittent blizzards. On the completion of this strip, 2,250,000 lb. of equipment, including 3,000 lb. of blasting dynamite, were ferried in. Such facts serve to underline the speed and intensity of the operations, which not only ensured a continuous supply of materials to the working shifts, but resulted in a significant drop in the freight rates. Between Mt. Joli (a base field on the south side of the St. Lawrence) and Burnt Creek (Schefferville) the freight rate was seventy-three cents a pound in 1947 when operations were beginning, but dropped to ten cents a pound by 1951. Between Mt. Joli and Wacouna, the rate was only five cents a pound in the latter year. These results were achieved with a miscellany of aircraft ranging from 'Norseman', DC–3's and DC–4's to the 'Packet' freighter already noted.

The second phase of development began with the completion of the railway in 1954. The first ore was shipped to Seven Islands in September of that year, and with the completion of the St. Lawrence Seaway some twenty million tons a year can now be shipped. The total cost of the project was approximately $470 million. The intensity of air operations current during the initial phase has now given way to more normal passenger and freight operations, still essentially on a non-scheduled basis. Since no large settlements or industrial developments are likely within the inhospitable territory of Labrador, air transport is likely to remain the vehicle of rapid communication between mine and civilization, restricting its operation to the carriage of prospectors mine officials and workers on the one hand, and the more valuable or perishable cargoes on the other. The continued survey of the Labrador and Ungava region and the possible extension of iron-ore mining provide future possibilities that may extend the exploitation of this vast territory.

We may sum up our discussion by suggesting the future possibilities in Northern Canada. Although permanent settlements exist within sub-Arctic Canada, it seems most unlikely that large-scale settlement will occur. The growth of big urban centres from which air transport may draw passenger revenues— the last phase in our plan on page 168—is a remote possibility. The accent is likely to be on exploitation rather than large-scale settlement, and even this must depend on the provision of surface carriers, without which little exploitation is possible. The aeroplane may find the minerals and assess the forest reserves, it may speed the establishment of mines and camps and provide a rapid link between them, but unless road, rail, or water navigation or some other form of transport like the tractor train be established, progress will be limited. Aircraft may help in establishing these links, as the examples we have considered have shown.

REFERENCES

1. Illingworth, F. 'Labrador's Iron-ore Airlift', *Flight*, June 1951.
2. Retty, J. A. 'Canada's Iron-ore Resources', *The Times Review of Industry*, January 1952.
3. *The Times Review of Industry*, 'Canada as a Uranium Producer', September 1953.
4. Washburn, A. L. 'Geography and the Arctic Lands', in Griffith Taylor, ed., *Geography in the Twentieth Century*, New York, 1951.

8

AIRPORT LOCATION

It has been said that aviation is the correlative use of three main elements : aircraft, airports and airways.[3] The key position of the airport depends upon the fact that it exists not only to enable aircraft to land and take-off safely, but also to facilitate the transfer of passengers and freight from one element to the other. Speed is a necessary feature of these operations, but safety and comfort are equally important. Safety includes not only movement on the airport itself, but in the airspace that surrounds it. Technical advance in aircraft design, together with the continuing upward progression of traffic density, means that airports must be planned with an eye to future conditions, i.e. they must be of an adequate size, and as near as possible to their actual and potential markets. As can be well imagined, no airport is perfect from all these angles : they are all compromises between conflicting requirements.

Although an airport should be planned as a unit, it is useful to remember that it consists of two main elements. In order that aircraft may operate safely, a field or runway is needed, together with tracks linking the take-off and landing path with service buildings. Secondly, provision must usually be made for the control and loading of the machines, maintenance and customs facilities, i.e. a group of service buildings must be constructed. Many variations between the provision of these two elements are possible. At one extreme we may find a simple 'airfield' or 'aerodrome' with a minimum of associated buildings. Jungle 'airstrips' often consist of a simple clearing only. Where airfields provide greater facilities, because of the type and density of traffic they serve, service buildings are a necessity. Such airfields are called 'airports' and may be further classified according to size and function.[4] The distinction between airfields and airports is, therefore, not unlike that made between harbours and ports in shipping circles. We shall be more concerned with the largest airports that handle both domestic and international traffic, e.g. London Airport or New York International, since locational problems are more sharply delineated in such instances. Apart from the airport itself, a wider penumbra of land is affected by its presence. Restrictions on building, road and rail development, and noise, are some of the more obvious influences, quite apart from the general question of land-use in the district.

We may distinguish three main groups of factors influencing the location of airports:

(a) Technical requirements of aircraft, landing aids, etc.
(b) Physical requirements of site.
(c) Economic requirements of site.

Fundamental is the clash between (a) and (b) on the one hand and (c) on the other. The former favour a large, unobstructed and nearly flat piece of ground, with good load-bearing properties and drainage, clear approaches and good meteorological conditions. Such needs suggest a site away from built-up zones. Economic desiderata favour such sites only in so far as land values are likely to be lower away from the city centre. Of greater importance is the proximity of the airport to the city it serves. Tiresome ground journeys from one to the other reduce the efficiency of the airport and of air travel generally, so that a site as near the city centre as possible is desirable. This is particularly true in the case of short-haul air routes, where the 'ground time' may represent a considerable proportion of the total time. *Table LIV* shows the distances of some of the world's airports from the cities they serve, and the significance of this data on short- and long-haul routes.

We may now consider airport location in more detail, bearing in mind not only the problems of the local site, but the broader relationships with traffic patterns and markets. The prime essential is the type of aircraft that will use the airport during its expected working life. At present that means the site must handle the largest projected type of fixed-wing aircraft, if it is to remain of

TABLE LIV

AIRPORT–CITY CENTRE DISTANCES AND TIME OF
GROUND JOURNEY

Airport	Distance from city centre (miles)	Time for journey airport–city (approx. limits in minutes)
London (Heathrow)	15	45– 90
New York International	17	75–120
Paris (Orly)	11	40– 60
Amsterdam (Schipol)	8	45– 90
Rome (Leonardo da Vinci)	22	60–100
Chicago (Midway)	10·5	30– 80
Montreal International	14	45– 90
Sydney	6·5	25

Example 1. Long-haul route. London–New York

Stage	Time hours	mins.
Victoria–London (Heathrow)		55
London Airport–New York International	7	35
New York International–New York (Fifth Avenue)	1	15
Total time	9	45

Ground time as a % of total time = 22%.

Example 2. Short-haul route. London–Amsterdam

Stage	Time hours	mins.
West London Air Terminal–London Airport (Heathrow)		45
London Airport–Schipol	1	5
Schipol–Amsterdam		45
Total time	2	35

Ground time as a % of total time = 58%

Source: *A.B.C. World Airways Guide*

international importance. Since aircraft performance is affected by elevation and meteorological conditions, these two elements must be taken into account in determining the acreage of concrete required. Fortunately, most large cities are situated in lowlands and elevation is not often critical. Climatic conditions are more important from this viewpoint in tropical areas, and can prove a determining factor. The ICAO[4] have laid down correction factors that take into account elevation and climatic—in this case, temperature—conditions. The standard is for a runway at sea level with an atmospheric temperature of 15°C. For elevation an addition of 7% in runway length per 1,000 ft. (300 metres) above mean sea level is suggested. This figure is then further corrected at a rate of 1% increase in runway length per 1°C. that the temperature exceeds the standard atmospheric temperature at that elevation. In the USA, the CAA recommends ½% increase per 1°F.; a slightly less rigorous correction. Turbojet airliners—which the international airport must now consider —are peculiarly sensitive to temperature changes, and the Douglas Aircraft Company have intimated that the DC–8's take-off distance under temperature conditions greater than standard is greater than the ICAO correction allows for.

In 1956[7] J. M. Ramsden considered the world's major airports in relation to the turbo-jet airliners, in particular the Douglas DC–8 and the Boeing 707. Of the fifty-eight leading airports, he found only one (Casablanca Nouasseur) capable of handling these machines with 100% regularity on every day of the year. Not only were many airport runways deficient in length, but the great weight of these aircraft demanded heavy bearing surfaces. *Table LV* gives the latest review of the situation with respect to London and New York. Since 1956, both airports have been extended, yet London still appears to be marginally adequate.

From such data we may begin to picture the size of the airport and the length of its runways. London Airport covers some six square miles, and although it was completed in most respects in 1956 it is still being developed, particularly by the addition of a long haul building, and extension and modification of the runway layout. In 1964, plans were ready for work to begin on freight buildings in the south-west corner of the airport.

The area chosen for the airport should be as flat as possible, taking into account the drainage and the bearing properties of the subsoil. Ideally, the site should be free from buildings or

TABLE LV

AIRPORT SUITABILITY WITH RESPECT TO THE DOUGLAS DC–8
AND BOEING 707 AIRLINERS

Aircraft Characteristics	Aircraft	
	DC–8 (Series 30) (Both fitted with	Boeing 707–320 JT4A engines)
Gross take-off weight (lb.)	315,000	312,000
Runway length for take-off (ft.)*	9,650	10,700
Maximum landing weight (lb.)	207,000	207,000
L.C.N. (approx.)†	85	96

* Take-off distance over 35 ft. screens
† Load Classification Number—basic parameter taking into account weight, tyre pressure and undercarriage geometry and incorporating isolated single wheel loading

Airport Characteristics	Airport	
	London	New York
Actual max. runway length (ft.)	11,000	14,600
Elevation (ft. above sea level)	80	12
Temperature (average daily, for hottest month. Degrees C.)	19	29
Main runway strength	L.C.N. 100	100,000 lb.*

* Single isolated wheel loading

Source: *Flight International*

mineral workings that may require removing or filling in. Since most airports are away from city centres, the land taken over is often agricultural land and entails little demolition work, although the loss of good agricultural land is not to be taken lightly. Where possible, sources of good aggregate suitable for runway construction should be readily available. River terrace sites, such as London Airport, often prove extremely advantageous from this point of view, apart from the fact that terrace gravels make good bearing surfaces.

Meteorological data are extremely important. Indeed whole books have been written on this aspect of the subject alone.[2] Not only must the local conditions be appreciated, but the climatic regime of the region as a whole is vital if approach aids and airways are to be used to the best advantage. Visibility is a prime consideration, with fog and 'smog' the chief offenders. Broadly speaking, a site upwind of the city centre is an advantage, particularly if industrial smoke is a feature of the city atmosphere. Extremely low-lying areas, except on the coast, are to be avoided, and local peculiarities of relief studied in case they produce fog pockets. Where necessary, the main airport should be situated in a different 'visibility region' from its alternative fields, so that at least one airport remains open most of the time. Heavy rain and snow may also reduce visibility, depending on the number and size of the droplets or flakes in the air.[6] Very heavy rain may reduce visibility to as little as 1,000 yards. Cloud may reduce the clear airspace over an airport to a few hundred feet, necessitating the use of approach aids. Low frontal cloud, convectional and stratiform clouds are the chief forms that give rise to such conditions, and their effects may be aggravated by local relief. The geographical distribution of visibility data has been discussed in Chapter 2, and *Figs. 4* and *5* summarize the material in map form.

Rainfall, except in so far as it affects visibility, is of less importance in temperate latitudes under average conditions. Heavy rainfall concentrated in a short space of time may cause flooding. Such precipitation is rare in the United Kingdom, but can be critical in tropical areas. The dry areas of the Earth's surface are often prone to this phenomenon, since the storms that do occur are frequently short-lived but very heavy. Bilham[1] has considered the incidence of heavy rainfall for the United Kingdom and elsewhere. The likelihood of more than one inch of rainfall falling in an hour in the United Kingdom works out at approximately one day in twenty years. *Table LVI* contrasts a British station with a tropical example as derived from Bilham's figures.

Snow may affect the operation of airports, and the incidence of snow cover will be important in colder climates and at high elevations.

Wind is relevant from two aspects, partly through the effect of the strongest winds on building strengths, and partly through the influence of wind on runway layout. The distribution of wind velocity over the year affects the layout of the major runways, taking into account also the influence of local relief, which may produce vertical currents and turbulence in the airport zone. The amount of 'crosswind' (angle the wind direction makes with

TABLE LVI

VALUE OF RAINFALL AS LIKELY AS NOT TO OCCUR ONCE
IN SPECIFIED PERIODS
(inches)

Period (years)	One hour		Two hours	
	Batavia	Calshot	Batavia	Calshot
1	2·16	0·44	2·91	0·63
5	2·75	0·63	3·80	0·87
10	3·00	(0·71)	(4·33)	(1·03)
50	(3·69)	(0·90)	(5·16)	(1·32)

( )= extrapolated values.
Records used—Batavia 1866–1936
Calshot 1920–1940

Source: E. G. Bilham[1]

the most favourable runway at any moment) that aircraft can
tolerate depends on the strength of the wind. From a study
of wind velocity frequencies the most suitable runway layout
may be devised to involve the least incidence of crosswind components.[2] In the United Kingdom, westerly winds prevail and
most main runways tend to run east–west in direction and can be
used on up to 84% of occasions.

Temperature and pressure changes both influence air density,
which, as we saw earlier, affects aircraft performance. Areas with
high temperatures or at high altitudes are the critical cases, but
pressure fluctuations are common in the cyclonic belts of the
world. For the determination of runway length at any proposed
airport site a knowledge of temperature and pressure ranges is
required. If the maximum temperature likely to be encountered
is calculated together with the associated pressure for the height
of the runway, a 'minimum density' can be ascertained upon
which aircraft take-off performance may be assessed. A further
allowance may then be made for the effects of temperature and
pressure on engine performance.

Equally relevant in matters of airfield location are other
geographical and economic factors. Most international airports
will handle traffic not only from the city, or cities, adjacent to
them, but as the result of their position traffic that is staging
through to other destinations. London Airport handles traffic for

London and the UK generally, but also European traffic destined
for North America. In spite of the enormous number of movements involved, most of the traffic will approach the airport
from a few well-defined directions. *Fig. 14* illustrates this pattern

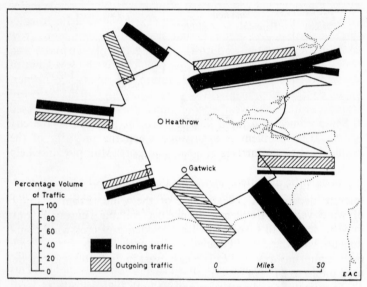

Figure 14 Volume of traffic using London's airports

for London Airport, and reveals that the bulk of the traffic
approaches from the south-east and the west. The site of an
airport will be influenced considerably by the pattern of routes
converging upon it, and should be placed so that a minimum of
traffic has to pass directly over the built-up city area. Such a
site not only avoids the possibility of accidents occurring over
densely populated areas, but may place the airport itself nearer the
overseas centres it serves. Indeed, the whole plan of the controlled airspace surrounding the airport will be affected.

When this fundamental pattern has been assessed, the question
may then be asked—is it economic to handle this traffic at one
site only, or should more than one airport be provided? There
are arguments to be found for both possibilities. Concentration
on one well-placed and extensive airport focuses activity to a

single point which endows certain advantages. More than one airport means more money and more land, and both are at a premium, e.g. London Airport cost £12,000,000 in the first five years of its development. Air traffic is markedly seasonal in character at present, so that with one site only, unused capacity at slack periods is likely to be at a minimum. Yet a single major airport supported only by a skeleton of alternative fields to cater for bad weather has serious limitations. Traffic continues to grow at an annual rate of about 15% at most major airports, and traffic control has become an acute problem. With the advent of big turbo-jet airliners, and, in the future, the supersonic airliner, traffic control remains a critical consideration. The problem will be most acute in bad weather conditions. We have already stressed the importance of a rapid link between the airport and the city served. This problem is aggravated when the majority of the traffic departs and arrives at a single airport. Multiple units help to spread the load.

It must be admitted, therefore, that when dealing with international airports of the first magnitude, multiple sites have much to recommend them. London illustrates the trend admirably. Originally, London Airport (supported temporarily by Northolt*) was planned as the main site, with Bovingdon, Blackbushe, Stansted and Hurn as diversion fields. None of the latter compares with London Airport in size or services available. This phase ended effectively with the Report of the Ministry of Civil Aviation on London's Airports in 1953.[5] This report recognized that London Airport alone could not be expected to handle all the traffic without substantial aid during peak periods. It proposed the extension of the field at Gatwick to the status of first main alternate, and Blackbushe as a second. Stansted was to be held as a reserve. Gatwick, which began operations in 1958, acts as London's main alternative airport, and took over some of the shorter internal and Continental services for which its southerly position is admirable, and serves as a base for charter operations. Since these decisions were taken, the performance characteristics of jet airliners, typified by the DC–8 and Boeing 707, have not improved the situation. We have already noted London Airport's marginal position with regard to these machines. The fact seemed inescapable that some further rethinking on the subject was warranted. Finally, in 1963 an inter-departmental committee

* Last service left Northolt on 30th October, 1954.

report[9] recommended the expansion of Stansted as the third London Airport. It might be added, perhaps, that London is not the only victim of air transport's rapid advance, for most of the world's major cities are facing similar problems.

The prospect of a further proliferation of airports on the already congested land around the world's big cities is not to be accepted lightly. Even the extension of existing sites would prove expensive. When the attempt is made to solve these difficulties, one is confronted with a dilemma. In the first place, by August 1956 orders had been placed for the big jets to the extent of 107 Boeing 707 and 110 Douglas DC–8 aircraft. Any airport that wished to remain in the front line had to be prepared to accept them and extensions to existing sites was unavoidable as a result.

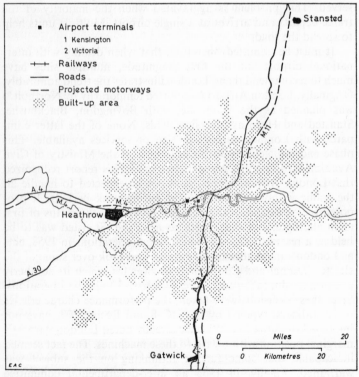

Figure 15 London's airport sites

If, in the second place, we look beyond this stage to the next generation of aircraft that will come into service approximately in the 1970–1980's, we are not justified in assuming that they will require similar runway requirements. The increasing efficiency of the turbo-jet engine, and the real possibility of a reduction in the take-off distance of future aircraft, suggest less stringent runway requirements. Eventually, vertical take-off will be achieved even with large machines, and enormous runways will no longer be required. Some may quarrel with the date when such machines will go into operation, but few people can dispute the trend.

Site values are, therefore, in flux at the present time. Future airports may move nearer the city they serve, provided problems such as noise can be overcome. In the interim period it seems that many international airports will have to be increased in size. Hand in hand with such growth must go improvements in airport–city communications. Many schemes have been mooted from monorails to helicopter services, but in the immediate future road transport looks like having to bear the brunt of the traffic.* Another problem occasioned by the big jets concerns the control of the airspace around the airport site. Since the number of alternative fields open to such machines is very limited, every effort must be made to use efficiently those that do exist, in order that the aircraft do not have to carry excessive fuel reserves in case of diversion. In spite of modern aids, flying control problems may make it necessary to divert a proportion of traffic, e.g. short-haul services, to other airports. Gatwick may have to handle more London traffic than is at present planned. From flying control's point of view, the direct distance between Gatwick and London Airport (twenty-five miles) is not over-generous, but it should prove enough to prevent interference between the traffic streams at the two sites. Gatwick has the further advantage that it is situated in a different 'weather zone' from London Airport. Precise records taken during December 1952–March 1953 have shown that 66% of all aircraft diverted from London Airport could have landed at Gatwick.[5]

Such then are some of the problems associated with the siting and development of the major international airports. We have considered only those adjacent to large cities, but included within the international category are airports like Gander, Newfoundland. These examples owe their existence purely to their strategic

* Note the exception of Gatwick, for which rail service is used.

position, for no large markets are locally available. Gander grew in importance as the Atlantic air routes became established. Its position as an outlier of the American continent makes it a vital refuelling point on the long ocean haul. Gander and similar airports like Lagens in the Azores, or Honolulu in Hawaii, are an interesting parallel with the steamer coaling stations, and like some of the latter are doomed to decline as aircraft performance progresses.

Secondary airports and airfields have rarely been the subject of extensive study. Many of them, particularly the larger ones administered by municipalities, play an important role in air transport. In the USA, municipal airports serve the domestic network, representing by far the largest proportion of the total. Even within the confines of the United Kingdom, enlightened municipalities, e.g. Manchester, Newcastle and Southend, are playing an important role in the provision of secondary airports. Our preoccupation with the major sites should not blind us to the part played by the smaller airports and airfields. They will prove an absorbing subject to anyone with the inclination to study them.

REFERENCES

1. Bilham, E. G. 'Classification of heavy falls in short periods', *British Rainfall*, 1935.
2. Durst, C. S. *Meteorology of Airfields*. M.O. 507, Met. Office, Air Ministry, 1949.
3. Froesch, C. 'The Planning and Engineering of Airports', *Society of Automotive Engineers*, December 1946.
4. ICAO *Airport Economics*. Circular 3, 1948.
   ICAO *International Standards and Recommended Practices*. Annex 14
5. Ministry of Civil Aviation. 'London's Airports'. Cmd. 8902, 1953.
   Ministry of Housing and Local Government, 'Report of an Inquiry into the proposed development of Gatwick Airport . Cmd. 9215, 1954.
   Ministry of Transport and Civil Aviation. 'Gatwick Airport'. Cmd. 9296, 1954.
6. Peterssen, S. *Weather Analysis and Forecasting*. 2 vols. (London and New York, 1940.) Vol. 1, 2nd Edition, 1956.
7. Ramsden, J. M. 'Impact of the Heavy Jets', *Flight*. May 1956.
8. 'Report of the London Airport Development Committee to the Minister of Transport and Civil Aviation', HMSO, August 1957.
9. *Report of the Inter-Departmental Committee on the Third London Airport*, HMSO, 1964.

APPENDIX

THE 'FIVE FREEDOMS' OF THE AIR

AN attempt was made at the International Civil Aviation Conference at Chicago in 1944 to establish certain operating rights for civil air transport operations. The result is embodied in the International Air Transport Agreement, Article I, Section 1, commonly known as the 'Five Freedoms' agreement. In brief, the freedoms state that a country grants other operators:

(1) The privilege to fly across its territory without landing.

(2) The privilege to land for non-traffic purposes.

(3) The privilege to put down passengers, mail and cargo taken on in the territory of the state whose nationality the aircraft possesses.

(4) The privilege to take on passengers, mail and cargo destined for the state whose nationality the aircraft possesses.

(5) The privilege to take on passengers, mail and cargo destined for the territory of any other contracting state and the privilege to put down passengers, mail and cargo coming from any such territory.

The first two are also contained in the International Air Services Transit Agreement (The 'Two Freedoms' Agreement). Most states grant the first two freedoms, while the remainder are negotiated by bilateral agreements.

BIBLIOGRAPHY

CHAPTER 1

M. R. Bonavia. *The Economics of Transport*. (London, 1936.)

R. O. Buchanan. 'Air Transport: some Preliminary Considerations', in *London Essays in Geography*. (1951.)

S. C. Gilfillan. 'World Projections for the Air Age'. *Survey and Mapping*. Vol. 6. (1946.)

R. E. Gross. 'The Transport Plane in Peace and War', *Air Affairs*. Vol. 3, No. 3. (1950.)

E. de Martonne. *Geographie Aérienne*. (Paris, 1948.)

E. F. Penrose. 'The Place of Transport in Economic and Political Geography', *Transport and Communications Review*. Vol. 5. (Dept. of Economic Affairs, United Nations, 1952.)

E. G. R. Taylor. *Geography in an Air Age*. (Royal Inst. of International Affairs, 1945.)

J. Parker Van Zandt. *The Geography of World Air Transport*. Volume I of *America faces the Air Age*. (Brookings Institution, Washington, 1944.)

CHAPTER 2

E. G. Bilham. *The Climate of the British Isles*. (London, 1938.)

C. E. P. Brooks and others. *Upper Winds over the World*. Geophysical Memoir No. 85 (Fifth No. Vol. 10). M.O. 499E, Meteorological Office, Air Ministry. (1950.)

G. A. Corby. 'The Airflow over Mountains—a review of current knowledge', *Quart. Journ. Royal Met. Soc.* Vol. 80. (1954.)

D. H. Johnson. 'The Jet Stream', *Weather*. Vol. 8, Nos. 9 to 11. (1953.)

D. Mason. 'Aircraft and Icing Research', *Weather*. Vol. 8, Nos. 8 and 9. (1953.)

Meteorological Office, *Equivalent Headwinds on some of the Principal Air Routes of the World*. Met. Report No. 7, Vol. 2, No. 2, M.O. 535b, Air Ministry. (1950.)

J. S. Sawyer. 'Pressure Pattern Flying', *Weather*. Vol. 3, No. 10. (1948.)

R. C. Sutcliffe. *Meteorology for Aviators*. M.O. 432, Met. Office, Air Ministry. (1953.)

CHAPTER 3

P. W. Brooks. 'Problems of Short Haul Air Transport', *Journ. Royal Aeronautical Society*. (1952.)

G. Fitzgerald. 'Tourist Fares', *Shell Aviation News*. (July 1954.)

'Economic Factors in Comet Operation'. *Flight*. (2nd May, 1952.)

M. J. Hardy. 'Transatlantic Air Freighting', *Air Freight*. (1955.)

P. G. Masefield. 'Some Economic Factors in Civil Aviation', Commonwealth and Empire Lecture, *Journ. Royal Aeronautical Society*. (1948.)

P. G. Masefield. 'Some Economic Factors of Air Transport Operation', Brancker Memorial Lecture, *Journ. Inst. of Transport*. (1951.)

United Nations Statistical Papers. *International Standard Definitions for Air Transport*. Series M, No. 8. (1950.)

A. Vernieurve. 'Helicopters in International Scheduled Operations', *Journ. Inst. of Transport*. (1955.)

CHAPTER 4

Air Transport Association of America. *Air Transport Facts and Figures*. (1954.)

G. Fitzgerald. 'World Trunk Air Routes', *Shell Aviation News*. Nos. 191 and 192. (1954.)

International Civil Aviation Organization. *Digest of Statistics*. Series TF-15, Traffic Flow. (March 1954.)

International Civil Aviation Organization. *Digest of Statistics*. Series T-12, Traffic. (1947–54.)

Political and Economic Planning. *International Air Transport*. No. 208 (1943.)

Roadcap and Associates. *World Airline Record*. 5th Edition. (Chicago, 1955.) Published annually.

H. E. Shenton. 'North Atlantic Traffic Statistics, 1952–54', *I.A.T.A. Bulletin No. 20*. (1954.)

United Nations Statistical Papers. *National and Per Capita Incomes of 70 Countries*. Series E, No. 1. (1950.)

United Nations Statistical Papers. *National Income and its Distribution in Under-developed Countries*. Series E, No. 3. (1951.)

United Nations Statistical Papers. *Statistics of National Income and Expenditure*. Series H, No. 8. (1955.)

CHAPTER 5

Air Research Bureau. *Internal Air Transport in Europe*. (Brussels, 1953.)

American Aviation, 'Russian Airline puts on New Look too' (Aeroflot). (29th August, 1955.)

British European Airways. *Report and Accounts*. (Annual.)

British Independent Air Transport Association. *Reports*. (Annual.)

British Overseas Airways Corporation. *Reports.* (Annual.)

Embassy of the USSR *Soviet Ambition Today.* Information Bull (1946.)

G. Fitzgerald. 'Passenger Survey', *Shell Aviation News.* (October 1955.)

Flight, 'The Soviet Airline Map'. (23rd July, 1954.)

P. G. Masefield. 'Recent Progress in British Air Transport', *British Association.* Advancement of Science, Vol. XII, No. 47. (1955.)

N. E. Rowe. 'Helicopter Transport in Great Britain', *I.A.T.A. Bulletin No. 16.* (1952.)

S. Wheatcroft. *The Economics of European Air Transport.* (Manchester University Press, 1956.)

CHAPTER 6

Civil Aeronautics Administration. *Inter-city Airline Passenger Traffic Pattern* (Washington, D.C., 1950.)

Civil Aeronautics Board. *Reports* (Annual). (Washington, D.C.)

Flight, 'City and Suburban Helicopters'. (22nd May, 1953.)

D'Arcy Harvey. 'Airline Passenger Traffic Pattern within the United States', *Journ. of Air Law and Commerce.* (1951.)

S. Klan. 'Twelve Thousand Company Planes', *Fortune.* (January 1956.)

W. A. Patterson. 'Stewardship of the Airlines by the Civil Aeronautics Board', *Journ. of Air Law and Commerce.* (1948.)

E. J. Taaffe. *The Air Passenger Hinterland of Chicago.* University of Chicago, Research Paper No. 24. (1952.)

E. J. Taaffe. 'Air Transportation and US Urban Distribution', *Geogr. Review.* (1956.)

CHAPTER 7

Air Affairs, 'Aviation in Africa'. (1947.)

W. A. M. Burden. *The Struggle for Airways in Latin America.* (New York Council on Foreign Relations, 1954.)

K. E. Callender. 'Airports and Aviation in Latin America', *Proc. of American Soc. of Civil Engineers*, Vol. 80. (1954.)

Flight, 'Far-Eastern Outlook'. (Growing momentum of Air Transport for S.E. Asia's Millions.) (6th March, 1953.)

D. M. Hocking and C. P. Haddon-Cave. *Air Transport in Australia.* (Sydney, 1951.)

G. Kimble and D. Good (Editors). *Geography of the Northlands.* (London and New York, 1955.)

J. G. Laight. 'Transportation Problems in Southern Africa', *Transport and Communications Review*, Vol. 6. (Dept. of Economic Affairs, United Nations. 1953.)

J. Pilditch. 'Air Developments in Canada', *New Commonwealth.* (31st October, 1955.)

M. M. F. Silva. *Geografia dos Transportes no Brazil.* (Rio de Janeiro, 1949.)

United Nations. 'Transport in Canada', *Transport and Communications Review*, Vol. 5. (Dept. of Economic Affairs, 1952.)

United Nations. 'Transport and Communications in Indonesia', *Transport and Communications Review*, Vol. 5. (Dept. of Economic Affairs, United Nations, 1952.)

I. S. Van Dongen. *The British East Africa Transport Complex*. University of Chicago, Research Paper No. 38. (1954.)

A. L. Washburn. *Geography and the Arctic Lands*, in Griffith Taylor's *Geography in the Twentieth Century*. (New York, 1951.)

CHAPTER 8

Air Transport and Airport Engineering, 'The Evolution of Idlewild'. (New York International.) (1946.)

Civil Aeronautics Administration. *City to Airport Highways*. (Washington, 1953.)

Civil Aeronautics Administration. *Statistical Handbook of Civil Aviation*. (Section II, Airports, pp. 3–14.) (Washington, 1955.)

D. A. Davies. 'Meteorology in relation to Airport Construction and Design', *Journ. of Inst. of Civil Engineers*. (1948.)

J. A. Dawson. 'Planning and Construction of Airfields', *Inst. Mech. Engineers*. Engineering Conference. (1951.)

C. S. Durst. *Meteorology of Airfields*. M.O. 507, Met. Office, Air Ministry. (1949.)

G. A. Gilbert. *Air Traffic Control*. (New York, 1945.)

Sir Frederick Handley Page. 'Towards Slower and Safer Flying, improved take-off and landing, and cheaper Airports.' 3rd Louis Bleriot Lecture. *Royal Aeronautical Soc.* (1950.)

International Civil Aviation Organization. *Airport Economics*. Circular 3. (1948.)

Manchester Guardian, 'Growth of an International Airport'. (Manchester.) (24th February, 1954.)

Meteorological Magazine, 'Fog at London Airport'. (1951.)

Ministry of Civil Aviation. *London's Airports*. Cmd. 8902. (1953.)

Ministry of Housing and Local Government. *Report of an Inquiry into the proposed development of Gatwick Airport*. Cmd. 9215. (1954.)

Ministry of Transport and Civil Aviation. *Gatwick Airport*. Cmd. 9296. (1954.)

New York Times, 'Idlewild Airport'. (11th January, 1956.)

J. M. Ramsden. 'Impact of the Heavy Jets', *Flight*. (14th May, 1956.)

K. R. Sealy. 'London's Airports and the Geography of Airport Location', *Geography*. Vol. XL. (1955.)

The following will be found useful:

The Aeroplane and Civil Aviation News. (Temple Press, Ltd., London.) (Weekly.)

Bradshaw's International Air Guide. (Henry Blacklock & Co., Ltd. London.) (Monthly.)

Flight International. (Iliffe & Sons, Ltd., London.) (Weekly.)

Jane's All the World's Aircraft. (London.) (Annual.)

INDEX